Doris Brett is a clinical psychologist, multi-award-winning poet and critically acclaimed memoirist and writer. Her books range through various genres, including therapeutic stories for children, fiction, memoir and poetry. Her latest book, *The Twelfth Raven*, is a memoir of her husband's devastating stroke and recovery.

Kerry Cue is a humorist, mathematician and journalist who has written for every major newspaper in Australia. Kerry is also the maths blogger Mathspig. She studied Science/Engineering at Melbourne University and taught maths and science for ten years before becoming a best-selling author of twenty humorous and educational books including *Life On a G-String* and *Australia Unbuttoned*. Her recent novel on American gun culture is *Target 91* (Penmore Press, 2019).

T0290223

DORIS BRETT & KERRY CUE

THE SUNDAY STORY CLUB

MACMILLAN
Pan Macmillan Australia

First published 2019 in Macmillan by Pan Macmillan Australia Pty Ltd
1 Market Street, Sydney, New South Wales, Australia, 2000

Cataloguing-in-Publication entry is available
from the National Library of Australia
http://catalogue.nla.gov.au

Typeset in 12/16 pt Sabon by Post Pre-press Group, Brisbane
Printed by McPherson's Printing Group

The author and the publisher have made every effort to contact copyright
holders for material used in this book. Any person or organisation
that may have been overlooked should contact the publisher.

When we started our salons, our aim was to create a space in which meaningful and authentic conversation could flourish. It would be an antidote to the rushed conversations or brief electronic communications with which our era is filled. The salons have been more wildly joyful, moving, uplifting and just plain wonderful than even we could imagine. The stories that have emerged from them have enriched us all and we want to dedicate this book to all the women who have so generously shared stories in the salons over the years and to all future salon participants, wherever they may be.

CONTENTS

INTRODUCTION

Ironically, considering how strongly we advocate face-to-face contact, the two of us met online. It was 2014 and Doris had just published a memoir, *The Twelfth Raven*, recounting her husband Martin's devastating stroke and extraordinary recovery. That same year, Kerry had established a website, Sibylesque, dedicated to breaking down the female stereotypes of age, size, marital status and so on. Kerry reviewed *The Twelfth Raven* on Sibylesque then emailed Doris with a link to the review; Doris replied with an invitation to her book launch. We didn't have much time to talk at the event, so we agreed to meet for lunch at a cafe halfway between our two homes.

At that first meeting, we realised that we were unalike in many ways: Doris is a psychologist, author, poet and psychotherapist with a Jewish heritage, while Kerry is a humorist, journalist, author and mathematician of Irish-Catholic background (now a sworn atheist). But we shared a few significant traits: curiosity, creativity and, importantly, a love of stories. We also discovered a mutual dislike of meaningless social chitchat, both of us preferring in-depth, meaningful conversation. This sparked an

1

idea: we should organise a salon at which people could actually engage in such conversations.

In early-eighteenth-century France, salons were formal gatherings in which people came together to discuss intellectual, philosophical and political topics. They became a venue for spirited intellectual discussion of the ideas of the day and allowed a variety of viewpoints to be heard, influencing many of the thinkers who shaped French society at the time. The salon we envisaged, however, would be of a different sort: instead of discussing the weighty topics of the day, we would discuss something even more weighty: our *inner* worlds. We would share the stories of ourselves.

We are all made of stories. The stories we tell ourselves about who we are, who others are and what the world is become our reality. The brain has, in fact, been described by neuroscientists as a 'story-making machine'.

At an evolutionary level, the storytelling tool of language has been crucial to the ascendency of the human race. As a relatively weak creature without a tough hide, poisonous spurs, claws, or even an ability to run faster than our predators, we could never have survived, let alone thrived, without our ability to turn experiences into words. The development of oral and, later, written language enabled us to pass on what we had deduced from useful experiences, to share our knowledge. Stories about our experiences, and the events surrounding them, allowed us to communicate what mistakes we had made, what we had already tried and discarded, and also what flare of creative impulse had led us to solutions.

In humans' earliest days, stories would have been told around campfires at night, during the repetitive work of collecting berries or sharpening flints, during tribal or religious ceremonies, during the walks from one campsite to another, the building of shelters, the preparing of meals or one of the myriad other occasions when people joined together in work or leisure and shared their individual experiences as well as the larger stories of their people.

In the 21st century, however, the context of personal storytelling has shifted radically, as has the means of communication. Today, instead of exchanging stories in the relaxed context of a leisurely walk or a shared task, stories are told through screens. The screens are physical, of course – the screens of the computer or smartphone – but they are also psychological, in the sense that the screen also functions as a mask. On social networking platforms such as Facebook, Twitter, Instagram and so on, users are creating images of the self intended for public – and, often, competitive – viewing. These short, pithy communications are sound bites rather than stories, designed to display the idealised rather than the actual self.

We are primed to be alert to, and aware of, what others think about us. Our earliest sense of self comes from the 'stories' that others tell us about ourselves. As toddlers we might learn that we are a 'good' girl or boy if we don't make a fuss, or a 'brave' girl or boy if we don't cry when we fall over. These stories told to us by others are eventually internalised as the stories we tell ourselves about ourselves. How we view ourselves and our lives thus depends on our 'self stories' and we tend to see these as fixed and immutable – until, perhaps, we tell them aloud. The response we see in listeners' eyes, the questions they

3

ask, the emotions that are aroused by them can change the way we see our own stories and, therefore, the way we see ourselves. But for that we need face-to-face communication.

For much of humankind's history, the only way we *could* communicate with each other was face to face; literacy was rare, and there were no telephones or video screens. Now, though, it is a common sight to see people facing each other across a table but with their gazes directed downwards to the ever-present screens. Communication technology might have conquered the challenges of physical distance, but it is increasing our emotional distance from each other. It is this distance we hoped to overcome through our salon.

When we first decided to run a salon, we agreed that we should establish a formal structure framed around pre-determined discussion questions. We wanted to ensure that every participant would have an opportunity to respond to the questions and have their story heard. We knew, too, that a crucial part of that structure would be the discussion questions themselves. We each had some experience in running workshops, facilitating conversations and interviewing people – Kerry as a journalist and Doris through her work as a psychotherapist. We were both accustomed to asking questions and making meaning of personal narratives. We wanted to create questions that were intriguing, that invited people to explore and discover. The questions could be playful or serious but, whichever they were, we wanted them to be questions that would make people stop and think. We called our salon the Sibyls' Salon, in celebration of the women who were revered as sages and oracles in ancient times. Michelangelo painted five such women on the ceiling of the Sistine Chapel. The best-known sibyl presided over the Temple of Apollo at Delphi from 650 BC. The words *Know Thyself* were inscribed in stone in the forecourt.

We decided that for our salons, we would focus on women over forty. Over the years of running our salons, ages have ranged from women in their early forties to women in their late seventies with most of us landing somewhere around our sixties.

We sent out invitations to friends and acquaintances who would not have met each other before. We wanted to avoid bringing together close friends, as we thought they would know each other so well that the answers elicited by the questions would already be familiar. (As it turned out, we found through the succeeding salons that not only are close friends surprised by the answers that emerge from the discussion questions, often the speakers themselves are surprised by what they discover about themselves.)

And so, on a Sunday afternoon not too long after our initial conversation, ten participants gathered for the first salon. They sat looking at each other rather warily – a group of strangers, not knowing exactly what was to come. Well, neither did we.

In our pre-salon discussions we had thought that we would need an ice-breaker, something to help people relax and let down their guard. We devised two: one involved writing down a 'guilty pleasure' or 'bizarre passion' on pieces of paper we handed out, and the other involved a group singalong to printed lyrics. Both activities fizzled – the two 'warm-ups' had prompted laughter, but the group still seemed awkward with each other. And so we shelved all of that and just got straight onto the discussion questions. It turned out that it wasn't necessary to contrive a bond between the salon's participants. People's responses to the discussion questions created the bond. Some responses were hysterical and the laughter was spontaneous. Some answers were moving and the group responded in kind. Above all, the answers were honest and human, and the shared experience of listening to others tell their stories wove its binding spell through us all.

In the average salon, we will end up hearing about twenty stories. Let us give you a peek into a typical salon.

It's a Sunday afternoon and a varied group of women is sitting in an assortment of chairs around a coffee table in a comfortable living room. The invitations went out a few weeks ago, with the two discussion questions included. The first is:

As you think, so you become . . . Our busy minds are forever jumping to conclusions, manufacturing and interpreting signs that aren't there.

Epictetus

What conclusions have you jumped to, walked up to, or taken on without even realising? And how have these conclusions affected your life?

The room is silent. We are listening to the storyteller.

. . . I'm sorry. I didn't mean to cry. But the salons have given me the opportunity to look back and think about my life. I've been tearful today because this question prompted me to talk to my partner

about relationships. It brought up all the self-doubt in me about my first marriage, about jumping to conclusions about marriage: how you get married and you think that means you can trust the person you marry – with money, with everything – even when that person isn't really trustworthy. It made me think about the roller-coaster ride I was on in that marriage and how I knew I had to leave it – which I did as soon as I was secure in my job. Walking out was like a rebirth in the sense that the external chains were lifted off me. But I have realised that some internal chains are still there. The marriage is behind me, but the self-doubt has remained. I ask myself: How can things be going so well now? It's almost as if I'm trying to predict the next catastrophe so I can protect myself from it. I don't talk to anyone about these feelings outside of the salons . . .

There are murmurs of empathy, recognition, heads nodding. For many of us this story resonates with something in our own lives: the self-doubt; the person who proved unworthy of our trust; the pain and uncertainty that comes with tearing up life plan A or B or C to walk off into the unknown.

We each take a moment to digest the story before sharing some responses to it. We talk about the assumptions built into the concept of 'marriage', the happy-ever-after fantasy and the 'prince' devoid of his shining armour or trusty white steed.

Not only does the storyteller gain insight into her own life through conjuring into words a sometimes deeply buried experience with all its conflicting emotions, the sharing of the story often invites others to abandon a carefully thought-through anecdote to spontaneously tell a story that has forced its way into their conscious thoughts while listening to another's tale. Some of these stories have us weak with laughter. Some are tragic. Some are inspirational.

It's time for another story.

. . . My dermatologist scrutinised the small, faint mark near my lip carefully and made her pronouncement. 'I think it's just ordinary sun damage. There's a possibility it might be a basal cell cancer (BCC) but I don't want to do a biopsy because I don't want to risk scarring you.' She was calmly confident as she went on to prescribe a cream which I was to use just in case it was a BCC.

That night I applied the cream without a second thought.

Later still that night, I dreamed. I was on a tram trying to get somewhere. But it was the wrong tram and with that feeling of foreboding that dreams channel so well, I understood that if I didn't get off this tram, and fast, something bad was going to happen. I woke slightly breathless with the panic of the dream, and the intense feeling of wrongness clinging to me. I understood immediately that it had to be about the cream and my dermatologist.

It was only then that I realised that 'I don't want to do a biopsy because I don't want to risk scarring you' was an utterly inappropriate thing to say on any occasion when the diagnosis was unclear. I needed a new dermatologist.

My *new dermatologist looked at the spot. 'I'm certain that it's a basal cell cancer,' he said. 'I'll do a biopsy to confirm it.'*

The phone call came a day later – it was indeed a BCC and an appointment was made for surgery. I was about to have a chunk cut out of my lip.

It was a confronting thought. Would my lips look distorted – the kind of distorted that causes people to ostentatiously avoid looking at you? Would I be able to smile properly? Would the expressiveness of my face change? When I looked in the mirror, would I still look like me? And what would other people see?

The BCC turned out to be much larger than expected. At the post-surgical check-up to have the many stitches taken out, my new dermatologist spontaneously said, 'It's a good thing you asked for a second opinion. That cream would have done nothing but disguise the problem. By the time you realised that the BCC was still there, it would have been much bigger still, and we would have had to take out a great deal more of your lip.'

Over the next few months my lip healed well, but if I had followed the first doctor's instructions, and not sought another opinion, it would have been a very different story.

It still chills me to think how close I came to that. My conscious mind, influenced by the absolute confidence displayed by my ex-dermatologist, jumped to the conclusion that she knew what she was doing. I am forever grateful that my unconscious mind worked its way through the night, to the opposite, and correct, conclusion.

There are nods of recognition as we talk about the 'face' we show to the world and what that means to us. And how we all too often take the functioning of our bodies for granted. Then the conversation shifts to the nature of premonitions or 'intuitive knowing'.

Several salon members have experienced premonitions, but it is so difficult to put faith in an ethereal dream, a fleeting vision or that little voice in your head. Yet some of these premonitions have come into being. How do we know whether to trust them? And how do we know who to trust? We have always been told not to trust strangers, and yet, counterintuitively, we in the salon trust each other, though for the most part we barely know each other. Ours is a bond forged by sharing and listening – really listening – to the deeply personal confessions, the screw-ups, the tragedies, the hysterical incidents, the triumphs, the messiness and the gloriousness of each of our lives. The free, safe space of the salon has given rise to an enormous wealth of stories and conversations – conversations about the struggles, failures, victories and uncertainties experienced by others. We have heard about lives quite different from our own. Perhaps it was a story about migration, becoming a mother, being stalked, stumbling by accident into one's true life, being abandoned as a child, not fitting the dominant stereotype society demands of you. We have listened to personal narratives of betrayal, courage, liberation, sacrifice, fear, joy, shame and endurance. Total strangers have shared stories they had never told anyone else before. We are constantly surprised – sometimes even by friends we've known for twenty years. How could we have not known this part of their real story? we wonder. We have also learned a great deal about ourselves, and that too is part of the joy of the salons. Very often, as the speaker tells her story, she sees patterns and connections that she had not previously seen. Often, the story we hear from a relative stranger brings us to a new perspective on some of the themes in our own lives.

One speaker, for instance, whose story is told in the chapter 'Being known', ended her story with a thought that had us all reflecting on our own experience of being known or not known. The speaker's mother had confessed to her daughter that she really didn't know her and the speaker concluded her story with this anecdote:

> *I was telling a friend of mine about this and she said to me: 'If you had been like that stranger in Paris and handed your mother a photo of your (inner) self, what would it have looked like?' The question stopped me in my tracks. What would my photo have looked like?*
>
> *And then, as I thought about it, it occurred to me that maybe we're really all going around like the man in Paris – handing out photos of ourselves that don't reflect what we look like on the outside, saying, 'Look, this is me, this is the real me,' and hoping someone will finally recognise us.*

Putting your story into words and telling it to an attentive audience helps you to reflect on and reassess your own life narrative. You didn't think you were that brave, but here you are in a salon and others are saying how brave you are. Even before the feedback from others, the simple act of retrieving that story from your memory banks and telling it can change the way you interpret the story and, in turn, the way you see yourself. Listening to other people's stories has the same effect. It enables us to see far beyond the external labels by which we are classified: middle-aged housewife; academic; political activist; accountant; mother. What we see instead is the rich, complex, tender interior of people's individual and deeply human lives.

Personal stories cut through stereotypical thinking and forge true connections and understanding. In this era of division and dislocation, truncated communication and curated images, it seems more important than ever to find ways of forging connections and promoting empathy and understanding. To listen to another person talk about their doubts and fears in the salon, to hear the emotion in their voice and see the expression on their face, is a profound experience. We leave the salon feeling euphoric and somehow renewed.

The salons have brought such a richness of connectivity and wisdom to us all, that we wanted to spread the word. We wanted to let others know about the salons and to guide them through the process of running, and being nourished by, their own salons. And so, *The Sunday Story Club* book was born.

We selected stories from a number of salons to give readers a sense of the depth and variety of discovery that is triggered by the discussion questions. All of the storytellers have given us permission to share their stories and we thank them for it. In turn, the storytellers have universally appreciated the opportunity to reflect on their own experience and commented on how much they have gained from it.

In the following pages, we share some of these stories,

before proffering some practical advice on how you can establish your own salon. And we hope that you, too, will experience the magic that comes with deep human connection.

WHO
ARE YOU?

'Who are YOU?' said the Caterpillar . . .
  'I – I hardly know, sir, just at present – at least I know
who I WAS when I got up this morning, but I think
I must have been changed several times since then.'
      Lewis Carroll, *Alice's Adventures in Wonderland*

**Who were you when you were eighteen
and is your present self different?**

From the time I was four years old – and, I imagine, before that too – my older sister told me almost every day that I was stupid, useless, ugly and disgusting. I was too young to know where that came from, so I simply took it in and absorbed it. But while I was despised by my sibling, I was adored by my parents (who adored both their children). I experienced both love and hatred in equal measure. How did these messages mix? They didn't. They remained completely separate, like water and oil in the same container – one could never dilute the other. Thus, I grew up with two selves inside me: the self that felt loved, accomplished and adventurous, and the self that felt worthless, foolish, ashamed and deeply inadequate.

By the time I reached adolescence, I was almost paralysed by shyness. I was too shy to ask a salesgirl for assistance; it would be a terrible imposition to ask her to waste her time and energy on me. If I had an appointment – say, with a dressmaker who was altering a dress to fit me – and I couldn't make it, I would be too shy to ring and reschedule. This shyness extended to social settings, too, where I was rendered almost mute.

On the other hand, I had close friendships. On a one-to-one basis with a friend, I was open, confident and funny. People felt comfortable talking to me about their problems. (I was referred to as 'the psychiatrist' on the page in the school yearbook where students write comments about classmates.) I was a bright student, and I had no trouble raising my hand in class and speaking up. To my mind, the classroom didn't count as a social situation.

Outside the classroom was another story. I could be talking and laughing with a good friend, but if another person joined us – even if it was someone I knew well – I would freeze. No longer relaxed and chatty, I would try desperately to become invisible. Of course, I never *felt* invisible. I felt as if everyone was focused on me – despising me, pitying me, wishing I were gone. It has been said that shyness is the mildest form of paranoia, meaning that the negative attention the shy person is convinced they are receiving, or will receive, in social situations is imaginary and magnified to the nth degree. It is true.

A schoolfriend tried to help me by explaining: 'You don't have to say much in a group. All you have to do is smile and nod occasionally at the right times and no-one will look twice at you.'

I practised this diligently. It didn't cure my shyness, but it did give me a way to cope with it.

I also discovered acting. My school put on plays every year. I was never nervous at auditions and I always scored a major role. I never had stage fright either. That might sound odd considering my shyness, but to me it made perfect sense: when I was acting, I wasn't me. If I wasn't me, I didn't have to apologise for taking up space in the world. I didn't have to worry about making conversation – my dialogue was scripted for me. I didn't have to worry about saying the wrong thing – the playwright had taken care of that. I didn't have to worry about what people thought of me, because on stage I was someone else. It was a joyous experience.

And so, having developed some coping mechanisms, my school years passed relatively uneventfully. I would feel at ease when alone with a friend but stayed silent in groups, focusing on nodding at appropriate moments and appearing relaxed while, inside, I wrestled with intense anxiety. Once, on a school bus trip, I found myself sitting next to a girl whom I had only encountered previously within a group. As we chatted animatedly, she suddenly stopped, looked at me and said, 'You are so not like yourself.'

Towards the end of my second last year of school, however, the balance I had achieved was suddenly threatened. Some of the subjects I wanted to study in year twelve weren't available at my school, but I had been offered a scholarship that would allow me to attend any school I wanted. I had to decide what I wanted more: to maintain the relative comfort of my status quo or to follow the study path in which I was interested. The latter course would mean starting a new school – a terrifying prospect. It was the first time I'd ever had to make such a major decision. My shyness had always been there, always a part of me. It had always felt impossible to defy it – I was compelled to do what it demanded of me. Now, I was being challenged to do the opposite.

And . . . I did it! When I first made the decision, I could hardly bear to think about what lay ahead, I was so frightened. But then I devised a strategy. No-one knew me at my new school, I reasoned; they didn't know shy me and they didn't know comfortable me. That meant I was free to create a new me. In group situations, I would draw on my acting skills and pretend to be someone who expected to be liked. I studied the confident girls I knew – observing how they entered a room, their body language, their tone of voice, their facial expressions – and I modelled my behaviour on theirs. I was a good actor, and my strategy worked. I made friends easily at my new school. I was still terrified in groups, but no-one ever would have guessed.

After finishing school, I made the decision to go to a university interstate, once again entering a world where I knew no-one at all. By this time, I was eighteen. I was doing a good job of impersonating a confident young woman, but in reality I was still shy. I could now talk to shop assistants, though I hated making phone calls. I could function in groups, but they scared me. I simply assumed that this was just how I was and always would be, that it was as fixed as the colour of my eyes or my adult height.

And then, in my third year of university, the universe decided it was time I learned to swim the hard way. The 'deep end' into which I was thrown was a unit of the psychology subject I was studying. It was the 1970s; encounter groups were rife, the study of group dynamics was hot and the compulsory unit involved taking part in a 'leaderless group', which would meet for an hour every week for twenty sessions. The leaderless group was pioneered by Wilfred Bion, a psychoanalyst, as a way of studying unconscious processes. There were papers written about it, but we were not supposed to read them – we were simply meant to experience the group then write an essay in which we would make sense of our experiences.

My classmates and I embarked on the experience with virtually no understanding of group dynamics of any sort, let alone leaderless groups. We were told that the only task of the group was to observe itself being a group. We were not told how to do this, nor were we told what processes to look for. Our instructions were brief, bland and baffling – study the group.

Initially we felt enthusiastic, if totally confused. The lecturer in charge of the course – who would also mark our essays – was part of the group but refused to act as its leader, despite our repeated appeals to him. When we asked what we were supposed to do, he said it was up to us. When we asked how we were supposed to do it, he said it was up to us. He basically remained silent throughout the sessions. It really was up to us.

The confident ones, the 'natural leaders', spoke up, suggesting things we could do – topics we could discuss, structures we could impose on the group, formats for the sessions. These suggestions were met with initial enthusiasm, which almost immediately subsided as we realised that, whatever it was they were suggesting, it was we who would have to do it and we didn't know how to do it – or even if we should be doing it. Even the strongest suggestion by the most dominant member of the group lasted no longer than a handful of minutes. Throughout all this, I said nothing. And continued to say nothing. It was excruciating. Pretending didn't work in a group like this. I was stuck with being who I was.

After the initial flurries of talk in the first few sessions, the group started falling into painful silences. People spoke up and were contradicted. People who didn't speak were challenged to speak. Some people blurted. Some were so hesitant that they never managed to say what they had intended. Some people wouldn't shut up. Some refused to speak, no matter how much pressure was put on them. Some sought approval. Some just wanted to shoot down anything that was proposed. Some wanted to take control. Some wanted to be invisible. Some people formed alliances, which quickly dissolved. Some stuck with each other as if super-glued together. Some people grew angry. Some grew tearful. Some sat with stony faces. Some wore expressions of contempt. But we all suffered. We all hated group time with a passion. At the end of the group, we would spill out of the classroom and, in contrast to the long and tortuous group silences, we couldn't stop talking. The relief of being outside the group was making our mouths move at a rate just below the speed of light.

We thought about the group constantly. It plagued us. We knew there had to be some way of figuring it out. We knew that at some point, it would suddenly all come together – we would know what we were supposed to do and how we were supposed to do it. But in session after session we struggled. We didn't have a clue what we were supposed to do, but we seemed to know what we weren't supposed to do; suggestion after suggestion was soundly, and sometimes harshly, quashed. Even the most outspoken members of the group grew subdued. The pressure on the silent ones increased.

Finally, about halfway through the life of the group, I gave in. Staying quiet, with the wrath of the group focused on me for not participating, was just too unbearable. I started talking. I made comments, asked questions, responded to people. I had spoken up in groups before, but this felt vastly different. This was like one of those dreams in which you discover you are naked. In this version of the dream, there was something I had to retrieve, but to do so meant walking through a crowd naked. I had to choose whether to hide – which would be safer but meant I would not achieve my objective – or to walk naked past the staring eyes to get what I had come for. Finally, *finally*, I had chosen to walk naked through the crowd. And to my astonishment, I discovered that what I had come to retrieve was myself.

I titled the essay I wrote about the group 'Waiting for the Magical Happening'. We had all started the unit in a state of both intense confusion and high expectation: a state guaranteed to produce an equally high level of tension. We had been handed a mystery – the equivalent of that old Russian fairytale titled 'Go I Know Not Whither and Fetch I Know Not What'. We all believed that, in the course of the group's sessions, we would find out where to go and that what we brought back would be a changed group – the group of our imagination: cohesive, purposeful and one in which we each fitted. In reality, though, we tried 'going' in all kinds of directions as a group, but we never brought back anything other than the group we had started with. And yet we all believed that the change had to happen, *would* happen; that, somehow, whether through a blinding flash of insight, the grinding gears of time or the hand of God reaching down to touch it, the group would be transformed. It was not.

Group members took varied amounts of time to process this knowledge. Some believed right up to the last moments of the group that it would change. Some recognised, around the three-quarter mark, that the group was not going to change. I was one of those. Recognising that it was not going to change was an initially depressing experience and even an enraging one – what on earth were we supposed to do with this? How could we get something out of a group that stubbornly remained as directionless as it had been from the beginning?

At about the speed of paint drying, I began to realise two things: first, that the group wasn't going to change; and second, that what could change was the way I experienced and responded to the group. When that understanding finally coalesced, it was revelatory. I couldn't control everything that happened to me – that would require godlike powers – but I did have the power to shape how I experienced what happened to me. The knowledge was both liberating and terrifying: liberating, because it meant there were choices and I could make them, and terrifying, because it meant there were choices and I could make them. In short, I was responsible for my own life.

Over the next year, experience after experience pushed me to keep recognising that fact: I had to take responsibility for me – for the choices I made, for the reactions I had, for what I took into my life. Over those twelve months, as that knowledge became a part of me, everything changed – most significantly, my relationship with my sister.

All our lives, my sister and I had been engaged in a dance. I would tolerate her cruelty for long periods of time, until it became too much and I would turn away. When I turned away, she would seduce me back. I would return and the dance would continue. She needed an acolyte. I needed to believe that, one day, she would love me.

In the year after the group, the cycle began as usual, but this time with a different ending. Instead of turning away to evade her cruelty, I looked it in the face. I really looked. And what I saw was that my sister would never love me. That in fact she hated me and always had. She had been this way since my earliest memories. I couldn't change her any more than I could change the group.

This time, when I turned away, it was a true letting-go. I not only let her go externally, I let her go internally. On the few occasions I had talked to friends about my relationship with my sister, I would find myself close to tears. They were tears of sadness, but they were also tears of shame. I felt ashamed that my sister didn't love me. But as that year progressed, I was able to talk about her without crying. I was able to think of her without shame. I was sad when I thought about her, but it was no longer an overwhelming sadness. I began to feel stronger than I had ever felt. In groups, I spoke up with a confidence that was truly startling to me. Week by week, I was doing things that I had never dreamed I was capable of. It was a profound and exhilarating change.

In those days, I travelled by tram a lot. It was a time when tickets were purchased from the conductors on board. Each ticket had a motto – a wise or pithy saying for the day. Of the thousands of mottos I read on my tram tickets, only one ever stayed with me. It was printed on a ticket I bought in my early teens and it read: 'We become like those we habitually admire.' It had stuck indelibly in my mind, but it had never occurred to me to wonder why.

I thought about it now. I had initially only seen its

surface – that you might want to wear the same hairstyle as a movie star you admired, for instance. Once I began to reflect more deeply on it, I realised that 'becoming like the people we admire' is a wish to make ourselves over in their image – to incorporate them, take them into ourselves. If you take out the words 'habitually admire' and replace them with 'people who matter most to us', it then becomes a statement of a profound human truth. As children, we form ourselves according to the building materials given us by the people who matter most to us – our families. If we have a loving parent, their voice becomes our own internalised loving voice, with which we praise and appreciate ourselves. If we have a critical parent, we take their voice into ourselves too, so that it becomes our own voice criticising and belittling ourselves.

I realised that in letting go of my sister, I had also let go of the internal voice – my sister's – which told me every day that I was ugly, stupid and awkward, and that there was no place for me in the world. Without understanding it, without even knowing it, I had chosen to make that voice a part of myself. And now I could choose not to.

In the years following, I found that I could step into groups with ease, that groups sometimes looked to me for leadership and I was comfortable with that too. Public speaking held no terror for me – I could talk to groups of three or 300 and enjoy the experience. I had never consciously connected my crippling shyness with the messages I had absorbed from my sister, but now I could see that this was where it had formed.

Traces of shyness remained – I hated asking people for favours that others found natural and self-promotion felt like doing surgery on myself with a rusty knife, but these were effectively pale wisps of cloud in a sky that had once been filled with thunderheads. For the first time in my life, I felt truly at home in myself.

About nine months after the group had ended, I ran into an acquaintance. I had met her briefly when she had visited friends I was staying with the year before. We exchanged the standard greetings and then she stood back and simply looked at me.

'What's happened to you?' she said. 'Something's happened to you.'

I was startled to the point of being shaken by the immediacy and certainty of her statement. My style of clothing hadn't changed. My hair hadn't changed. But something deeply internal *had* changed and she could see it as clearly as if there was a nimbus of light surrounding me.

She could see what, for years, I had not even known that I had lost. She could see that I had found myself.

SERENDIPITY

Serendipity . . . You will understand it better by the derivation than by the definition. I once read a silly fairytale, called 'The Three Princes of Serendip': as their Highnesses travelled, they were always making discoveries, by accidents and sagacity, of things which they were not in quest of.

Horace Walpole

**Have you experienced serendipitous events,
whether large or small, in your life?**

I lied. I lied about what I felt, what I thought, what I wanted, what I had done, what I was doing and what I was planning to do. I lied as a child, as a girl, as a young woman. I lied constantly, reflexively and eloquently.

My lies were focused around what I considered to be the most important things in life: status, success, who you knew, what you had achieved. But my mother took it one step further. She didn't just lie about important matters; she lied about everything, no matter how trivial. She would say, for instance, that she had been shopping at Target when really she had gone to Woolworths. Nobody in the family, including my mother, had any strong beliefs about the relative value of either Target or Woolworths; it affected nothing and no-one. And yet my mother would still lie about it. Even if you had seen her entering Woolworths, she would still insist vehemently that you had seen her at Target.

My parents had started dating in high school. Two years after my mother graduated, she went to the doctor about a tummy bug and discovered that she was pregnant. Her conservative Baptist parents were outraged. Marriage was the only option and it happened quickly.

My brother's birth was a disappointment – my mother had her heart set on a girl. She was determined but her body was unwilling. Years of unsuccessful attempts to conceive again followed, including four miscarriages. Finally, two years before my brother went away to university, I was born.

My father's work took us from city to city, each hoped-for promotion turning out to be merely a sideways shift. Eventually we landed in California, where the company finally made it clear to my father that he was never going to rise beyond the ranks of middle management. We lived in a relatively affluent part of Sacramento. Our neighbourhood was not the wealthiest but neither was it aspirational – people living 'here' until they could live 'there'. The people who lived in our area felt they were already there. My parents were never 'there'; they were too busy running, like the Red Queen in *Alice's Adventures in Wonderland*, in order to simply stay in place. I was never 'there' either – I was too busy working out the next place I was supposed to be. Our house was a nice house on a nice street. I went to a private school. We were always dressed well. We looked good in the way that a shiny red apple looks good until you bite into it and find the rot.

Behind our gleaming facade was quite a different reality. My father was a violent, alcoholic gambler. And he didn't have to be drunk to be violent; anything could cause him to snap. To be in his presence was to tread a high-wire. If we stay quiet, he won't yell; if we don't catch his eye, he won't hit . . . I went to ridiculous lengths to avoid angering him. Instead of going to the bathroom in the night, for example, I would pee into a container and pour it out of the window, so fearful was I of disturbing his sleep.

My mother believed with an almost fanatical certainty that the reason she had ended up with my father was because she had not continued her schooling and had taken on a low-status job. A whole host of better, higher-earning marriage partners had been denied to her because of her 'lowly' status. She was adamant that I must do whatever it took to avoid marrying someone like my father.

Her first rule was 'pretty'. I was prettier than her, she said, which would help me to snare a better man. But while pretty was good, it was not enough. I had to be the prettiest. She set about achieving this goal with a vengeance. Years later, the mother of one of my schoolfriends told me that when she saw me on my first day of kindergarten, she had to stop herself from staring – I had the head of Marilyn Monroe on the body of a kindergartener. I was 'styled' even when I was five. By the time I was six years old, my mother had taken me to the hairdresser for a full head of highlights. She set my hair in rollers after each wash. I went to school looking like a pageant contestant. I hated it with a passion, but that didn't matter.

Of course, pretty also meant slim. I was not a fat child – I had a sturdy, athletic build, which I was perfectly comfortable with. When I turned fourteen, however, my mother announced that she was putting me on my first diet. I mightn't have thought I was fat but she did. And so I lost weight. You do when you eat only grapefruit or hard-boiled eggs or cabbage soup or whatever the latest fad diet recommended. My mother was thrilled with my weight loss. She took me out on a shopping spree – new clothes, new accessories, new everything. This time

I wasn't complaining. Now that I was a teenager, I loved dressing up.

My weight crept up again, of course. Once more, my mother put me on a diet. I lost the weight and again was rewarded with a wonderful shopping trip. The pattern repeated regularly and soon I didn't need shopping trips as reinforcement. I believed: to look good you had to be slim, and crash diets were the way to achieve this. For decades I fought a war with my body, which kept stubbornly returning to its natural weight.

Appearance was everything to my mother. She took care with her own appearance, but she had never been startlingly beautiful and was herself overweight. I was to be everything she had wanted to be – her second chance. The right hair, the right looks, the right clothes were what hooked a rich husband.

This is not to say that my mother dismissed the importance of education. She considered university essential. The higher your academic qualifications, she insisted, the better chance you had of landing a doctor or lawyer. That I could become a doctor or lawyer myself didn't enter into it. An academic qualification was not a goal in itself. Neither was a career.

I was naturally pretty and could make myself even prettier with the investment of time. Academically, I wasn't a rocket scientist, but I was bright. My problem was application. I was constantly distracted by the violence at home and the fear and hyper-alertness to danger it engendered. Add to that the constant self-monitoring that presenting a perfect image required and I had little time to focus on my studies. And since no-one outside of examiners, teachers or employers ever asked to see physical proof of my academic achievements, it was easy to lie and exaggerate my achievements – and it got even easier as I grew older. If you tell someone that you're doing postgraduate study, they are very unlikely to call up the institution in question to check. And so I told people I was doing a master's degree. No-one questioned me. They just assumed I was smart – a career woman on the way up.

Lying seemed normal to me. I learned it early. I was small, I was vulnerable and I was scared. It was my mother's preferred tool of survival and it seemed natural that I too should use it to keep myself safe – and 'safe' was a complex notion in my family. It didn't just mean safe from my father in the present; it also meant safe in the future, in which I had to avoid marrying someone like my father. I became proficient at lying. And I found that most people wouldn't confront me on my lies. They would either believe them or ignore them. Sometimes they would avoid me, but no-one ever looked me in the eye and called me a liar. I don't know why not. Perhaps because my lies weren't nasty lies; there was no malice in them. They were purely about my survival and my need to feel worthwhile. Or maybe it was because, as well as being a liar, I was a nice person.

I liked helping people. I liked pleasing them. And I was soft-hearted. I had a lot of friends – though very few genuinely close friends. It's difficult to have authentic friends when you're not authentic yourself, and the energy that it takes to disguise yourself is energy taken away from the relationship. I sometimes envied people who seemed to make close friends effortlessly, though from the outside I probably looked as if I were that sort of person myself. I led the kind of social life that was normal for my set of friends at that time – socialising with girlfriends, but always with an eye out for a boy.

I knew exactly what I was looking for in a boyfriend. That it was also exactly what my mother was looking for in a future-son-in-law was no coincidence – I had taken in her lessons on how to secure a safe future from an age so young that I couldn't even remember when I first became aware of them. I knew exactly what I needed to look for. He had to come from a well-off family. He had to earn a lot of money. And he had to want to marry me. These were the only qualities that mattered.

I met my future husband at a party. He was the one looking slightly uncomfortable in a corner. I knew that his family was wealthy. They entertained lavishly and had the city's most prominent citizens on their guest lists. My husband-to-be had just graduated with a law degree from Yale. He was extremely bright and could have got a job anywhere, but he'd come home to Sacramento to be near his parents. He had been courted by all the top law firms in the city and had taken a job with the firm considered to be the crème de la crème. His friends assured me that he was on a fast track to partnership. The icing on the cake was that he had been so focused on his studies and work that his social life hadn't been a priority. He wasn't especially handsome, and he didn't have girls hanging around him. I was in one of my 'slim' phases – a blonde bombshell. It wasn't hard to dazzle him.

He was very close to his family. He saw them at least once a week and spoke with his mother more often than that. A lot of women would have found that off-putting, but I loved it. A close, loving family? I wanted it!

I considered it a bonus – the free steak knives that would come with the marriage.

For his part, my husband-to-be didn't know much about my family. Only the surface was on display and the surface looked, if not excellent, at least reasonable. And what he believed he was getting in a wife was not only a beautiful blonde but a highly educated career woman with sterling job prospects. His mother even privately voiced her concern that perhaps I might be *too* career-focused rather than the supportive partner she felt he needed. As I said, I was a good liar.

We got married. It was the wedding I'd always wanted: the stately old church awash with flowers; the minister who had known the family for decades; the flowing white dress that might as well have had 'happily ever after' embroidered on the hemline; the husband who gazed at his wife as if he couldn't quite believe how beautiful she looked; the family and friends who cheered when we entered the reception as husband and wife. And, somewhere underneath it all, the feeling that I was taking part in a play.

Once the wedding ended, it was as if time was reeling backwards, undoing things – going from the polished performance of the play to the messy rehearsals where the actors hadn't quite memorised their lines and stumbled through their reading. You could see that they were actors after all, and not the characters they portrayed. You could see who they really were.

One of the things I saw was that my husband was a compulsive truth-teller. He not only didn't know how to lie, he believed that it was essential to tell the truth. He didn't even understand white lies. If someone asked him

whether he liked their new car, for instance, he genuinely
believed that they wanted his honest opinion. 'Not worth
the money you paid for it,' he would say, not understanding that what they wanted from him was a white
lie: 'Looks great!' A compulsive truth-teller – who had
married a compulsive liar.

The other thing I discovered about my husband after
marriage was that he didn't see his job at the prestigious
law firm as a fast track to a lucrative partnership; he saw
it as a mere way station en route to what he really wanted
to do, which was help people. And what he really, *really*
wanted to do was help those people who couldn't afford
to pay for his help. So, after barely a handful of years at
the firm, he left for his dream job – a relatively low-paid
government job in which he could help people who
couldn't afford a private lawyer. His salary was a steady
and comfortable one, but there was no way it would
finance the lifestyle I'd thought I was marrying into – the
plush first-class-all-the-way lifestyle of a top lawyer's wife.

My husband also realised a few things about me after
marriage. If he wasn't who I'd thought he would be, he
was in for a similar shock about me. We both felt cheated.
We both felt angry. And so, for the worst reason in the
world, I fell pregnant very quickly – to keep us together.
A child provides a bridge between the parents, I reasoned.
My husband and I could stay on opposite sides of the
bridge – connected but also separate.

That first child turned out to be children plural – I
was pregnant with twins. They were a little premature,
although healthy, but their smallness made them seem
exceptionally fragile. I lived in a permanent state of
terror. Feeding was a nightmare. I didn't have enough

milk – another mark of failure, as I saw it – and they seemed to cry constantly. I would just manage to settle one when the other would start, setting off a fresh bout of tears from the first. Rocking, wheeling, pacifiers . . . nothing seemed to console them. I felt totally helpless. When I took them for walks in their double stroller, I would see other mothers cuddling babies in their slings or cooing to babies who looked up at them attentively. I felt like nothing. Less than nothing. Sleep was impossible. Almost everything seemed impossible.

My husband was studying for a higher degree as well as working at his more-than-full-time job. He was at the library studying until late at night and then left for work before the babies and I got up in the morning. I needed him desperately and he wasn't there.

Postnatal depression hit with a vengeance. I felt completely useless. I had no idea what I was doing. I had no models to follow. I had no instinctive sense of what good mothering meant – I had never experienced it. I didn't know what I was supposed to do. I didn't know what I was *not* supposed to do. I was in a constant state of strangely muffled panic that felt like having to run through deep water as fast as I could, knowing that if I couldn't run fast enough, something terrible was going to happen. And I couldn't run fast enough. Everything was a fog. I was a fog. And through the fog burned a steady resentment at my husband for not being there to help.

Nine months went by – it felt like nine years – in which I barely managed to put one foot in front of the other. And then I made a jaw-dropping discovery: I was pregnant again. I was terrified. I knew I could never cope. A baby doesn't know that, though, and grows on anyway.

Meeting my third child was an astonishment for me. He was such a contrast to the twins: a relaxed little soul, easily comforted and able to amuse himself happily for long periods of time. For the first time, I felt like a competent mother – I could meet his needs. The postnatal depression that had continued to dog me since the birth of the twins vanished.

Children had always been on the agenda for me. And it was always multiple children, not a single child. My brother had left home for university when I was barely old enough to speak and had never returned, not even for Christmas. I was effectively an only child. When I was young I'd been desperate to find my way in what was a confusing and often frightening world, but I had no way of distinguishing what was real from what was false, what was right from what was wrong. I was too frightened to approach my father and I couldn't trust my mother. There was no-one to ask, no-one to give me reliable feedback, no-one to offer sound reality-testing. If I'd had a sibling, there would have been that someone. I didn't trust myself, but one thing I could give my children was siblings, so that if I failed or was impossible or untrustworthy, as my mother had been, at least they would always have someone they could rely on. And with three children, I had done that.

But while I had succeeded on that front, my marriage was in a dismal state. The emotional climate between my husband and me veered between resignation and hatred. Resentment was the fulcrum upon which it rested. On the fleeting 'good' days, it climbed to the temperate region of resignation, but most days were weighted downwards into mutual hatred. My husband coped by shutting off and disappearing emotionally. I coped in my usual way, presenting a facade of Mother and Homemaker of the Year to the outside world while inwardly roiling in a toxic mess of rage and despair. I didn't know how I was going to keep going. But I had to keep going for the children. And there were many times when they were all that was keeping me alive.

My days were spent managing three very small and active children. By late afternoon, I was clock-watching, desperate for my husband to come home and help. He, in turn, would come home exhausted after a long and arduous workday. We were each demanding something the other couldn't give. But at least there was a light at the end of the tunnel: we were going to buy a house. The finances were finally in place. Our new home had enough room for our growing family, a swimming pool, and – with some redecorating – would be *House and Garden* cover-shot perfect. It wouldn't heal our marriage, but at least it could fester in beautiful surroundings. I would be living in the house of my dreams. It cost more than we'd intended to spend, but we could stretch to that amount. It was on the right street in the right neighbourhood with the right neighbours.

But shortly after we had taken possession and begun renovations, it was discovered that the land on which our perfect house stood was toxic. The toxins were hazardous to human health. They could spread with contact. They required specialist removal. Indeed, the whole house had to come down, the foundations had to be excavated, and then everything and anything left had to be scoured sterile. And that was the end of the dream home that we had paid for in money we couldn't get back.

It was devastating. And, in a small community, very public. We felt like fools, ashamed of being duped. We felt enraged. We made frenzied attempts to recover something, anything, from the financial fiasco, but it seemed impossible. People pitied us. People avoided us. People told us what we should have done long after the horse had bolted. People tut-tutted. People were sympathetic. But nobody helped us. My husband's parents had experienced a series of financial setbacks, so even they couldn't help us. We were desperate. We'd lost everything.

Somewhere in the depths of our misery, the realisation dawned: we were all we had – it was just us. And, even more slowly, I realised that when there was nowhere else to turn, my husband was there, a rock in the middle of a sucking tide. When I was terrified beyond words, he was the one who said, 'We'll get through this.' Through the months of chaos, we slowly, slowly began to hold on to each other.

It was while in the midst of this waking nightmare that one day, as I waited by the school gates at pick-up time, a mother whom I knew from shared play dates approached me.

After the requisite greetings, she looked me up and down as if to assess something, then said, 'You should come to my qi gong class.'

I stared back at her, startled. I'd never heard of qi gong. If I'd had to guess, I would have said it was an exotic fruit.

'Qi gong is a form of tai chi. It's about life energy.'

I backed away involuntarily – I had no life energy. 'Not my thing,' I said.

She was insistent. 'You need it.'

I shook my head, but she persisted.

42

'Please – just try it.'

Whether through a desire to please or because I was too tired to resist, I relented.

'Great!' she said. 'We can go tomorrow. But you have to promise one thing – you have to commit to six sessions before you decide whether or not to continue.'

And so I was dragged along to my first qi gong class. I hated it. And I also hated the fact that I couldn't do it. I dutifully attended six sessions, and by the sixth session I still felt like a clumsy fool. And then, purely because of the challenge to my ego, I became determined to master it. I went to class after class. And something strange happened.

Originally, the mastery of qi gong had sparked my competitive spirit, my wish to be the best. It was just another forum for competition – the prettiest girl, the most amazing mother, the star qi gong student. But gradually I began to realise it was more – much more. It was the breathing that got to me first. The instructor told us just to breathe: to notice our thoughts but not get involved in them, to breathe until eventually there was stillness. Initially this was impossible for me. But to my amazement, the instructor told me that was all right. I didn't have to 'get it' immediately. It was okay to be imperfect, to make mistakes. It was a revolutionary idea. Okay to be imperfect? No-one had ever said that to me before. Not being able to master the breathing didn't mean I was out of the game; it just meant I needed more time to find my way in. And I was allowed to take that time. Session by session, I kept breathing, just letting myself notice my thoughts, be curious about them, and let them go. And then one day it happened – I felt the stillness. It was the first time in my life I had ever been still.

I found myself breathing in all kinds of places. At home, when I was about to lose my temper over the mess on the floor. In traffic jams, stuck in a river of cars when I was late for appointments. And, startlingly, when I was on the verge of lying. Previously, I had done everything, including lying, reflexively, defensively; now, when I was breathing, I had the space to simply be. And in that space, I could actually see myself. Not as I was supposed to be, not as I wanted to be, but simply as I was. And what I saw when I saw myself was someone who was damaged. I had been aware of that damage all my life, of course – my lying had been the desperate attempt to slap a coat of paint, or a dozen, over it. But now, when I saw that damaged being, although my automatic response was to cover it up, disguise it, another part of me could, for the first time, accept the fact that maybe I didn't need to be perfect.

Week by week, I was changing. Each time I felt those familiar triggers – the comparison with others, the casual query about what I did, the glance at my outfit – all those red buttons that had once screamed: 'Lie! Make up something! Look brilliant!' – I would make a conscious effort to stop myself, to pause before responding, to try to tell the truth. It was incredibly difficult. I felt naked without my coat of lies. Naked in bright sunlight with every flaw revealed. But I kept trying. I kept doing it. I stumbled sometimes over the issue of white lies – was it permissible to lie if telling the truth would hurt someone? If so, always? Sometimes? Never? I tripped up regularly with the reflex of old habits. But the trip-ups became less regular, the reflex less automatic. Gradually, although it still required constant effort and invoked fear, it got easier. And as weeks and then months passed, it required less constant effort and scrutiny and less fear, although it was hard for me to know what the normal level of apprehension about revealing yourself to strangers or even good friends was. Did everyone feel some degree of fear and vulnerability?

Throughout it all, I kept doing qi gong. I kept breathing. I found more and more patches of stillness. Qi gong forced me to really sit with myself. To listen to my thoughts. To listen to myself and understand who I really was. I began to see that we are all imperfect, that it is part of the human condition and I, too, was allowed to be human. So were the people around me. So was my husband. I stopped feeling resentful. I stopped feeling like a victim. I stopped feeling enraged.

My husband noticed the changes at around the same time I did. He told me later that he first became aware of the change in atmosphere when he came home. Previously, walking into the house was akin to walking straight into the wall of resentment that surrounded me. His response had always been to mentally retreat, to shut off. Now the wall was gone. And when he crossed the threshold of our home, all of him wanted to come in rather than step away. Cautiously, tentatively, we both began to step forward.

I learned to embrace my marriage, and I began to see my husband with new eyes. He's not emotional or dramatic like me, but he's a very kind person. A genuinely decent person. And he's very forgiving, as long as you accept responsibility for your actions. He doesn't tolerate bullshit. And he's very grounded. He offers the stability that I had longed for and could never find in my childhood family.

We began to talk openly and honestly, in a way I'd never talked to anyone before. We talked about what we had each expected from our marriage and the disappointments and betrayals that we'd felt. We talked about lying and turning away and all the hurt we had each experienced. And we talked about the renewal that had come so unexpectedly.

My husband has seen me work hard to change myself and he admires that about me. I, in turn, have taught him that it's okay to be imperfect – he's always been too hard on himself. My softness has allowed him to treat himself more gently. He has always led a very moral and authentic life. In the beginning, I resented that because it was so contrary to what I was and what I felt capable of being. Now I am glad of it; it's what I want for myself. He knows exactly where I've come from and all the lies I've told, but now that he's seen me stripped of all pretence, he says I inspire him because he's seen the transformation I've undergone. We're there for each other. I feel safe with him in a way I've never felt with anyone. How ironic that, in my desperate effort to marry the wrong man, I accidentally married the right man.

I went back to university and studied interior design. I run my own business now. My clients are almost all women. Most people think that interior design is about what the latest trends are – minimalist versus shabby chic, rose versus red. That's not how I see it. For me, interior design really is about the interior: about who you are on the inside. I ask my clients questions they've never been asked before. What colour makes you smile? Where do you feel safest? What does comfort mean to you? Sometimes I recognise the answers because I've lived them.

Sometimes they open floodgates of talk and I can listen, really listen. Sometimes they will tell me that it's the first time they've said these things aloud, the first time someone has really listened, and I nod my head. I know.

I used to think that it was the serendipity of discovering qi gong that saved me, but now I wonder whether I would have been able to take up that opportunity if the toxic house hadn't, at the same time, catapulted me into the most desperate time of my life, when I was at rock bottom emotionally. If I hadn't been brought so low by that financial disaster, and if our predicament had not been so public, would that mother at the school gate have even suggested qi gong to me? If we hadn't lost all our savings in that house, would the terror have been enough to break through the wall I had constructed around myself and make me grab the line that qi gong was throwing me? I can't ever know for sure, but I believe that as well as giving me qi gong, serendipity also gave me that house. It dragged me kicking and screaming into confronting, unavoidably and without the shield of lies or disguises, the poison that ran through it – not just the poison on the inside, but the poison that was underground and invisible. I stumbled into the perfect metaphor for my life: that house, so beautiful on the outside and toxic on the inside – and in the end it saved me.

IDENTITY

What part of your own identity is very important
to you, especially if you've had to struggle to
establish, maintain and/or defend that part of
your identity at various stages of your life?

The part of my identity that I have had to fight for has also fought against me. I have fought it for most of my life. I've tried every way I could think of to control it, change it, bend it to my will. Sometimes I have succeeded, but I've always been aware that, when I do, it's a truce rather than a victory. And the worst aspect of it is that some wiser part of me believes that if I were truly strong, I wouldn't be fighting it at all, I would just let it be what it is. Alas, that wiser part of me never wins, because I am not strong enough to simply let it be what it naturally is; I am always trying to make it conform to what *I* want it to be. What I'm talking about, of course, is my hair.

When I was a little girl, I was an odd combination: a bookish tomboy. When I wasn't reading, I was riding my bike around the streets, climbing woodpiles in the yard and pretending to be a cowboy. I couldn't have cared less about my hair. In fact, I didn't care much about my appearance in general. Outside school I only ever wore jeans and T-shirts. I was irritated when I first had to wear a bra because that meant it took me two whole minutes more to get dressed. What a waste of time!

DORIS BRETT & KERRY CUE

And then, inevitably, I became a teenager. Suddenly appearance mattered – and hair in particular. With respect to hair, the rules were iron-clad. The only acceptable hairstyle was straight. Preferably with a bouncy turn-up at the ends. Preferably blonde. But always – most definitely and without exception – straight. This meant curly-haired girls like me had a problem. Or, as many of us thought, gazing at the polished, glossy, straight-haired teen magazine cover-girls, we *were* a problem.

We ironed our hair; we pulled at it with super-heated ironing tongs; we doused it with straightening chemicals that seared the insides of our nostrils and did heaven knows what to our hair; we slept with our hair wound around our heads and fastened with hard metal pins. (It didn't matter if we couldn't sleep very comfortably – all that mattered was that our hair would be straight in the morning.)

We became frightened of weather. Too hot and our hair went curly. Too cold and our hair went curly. Too damp and our hair went curly. Too foggy and our hair went curly. Too windy and our hair went wild and curly. We needed mild, sunny, frost-free, dew-free, wind-free, totally stable weather. And we lived in Melbourne. Good luck with that!

The state of our hair was an anxious undercurrent to our day. If we had managed to emerge from the house with it straight that morning, that was wonderful and afforded us a moment's relief as we looked in the mirror. But in half an hour's time, and every half-hour after that, the internal question assailed us: was it still straight?

One day, when I was thirteen, a friend and I went off to the cinema to see the premiere of *Dr Zhivago*, starring

Julie Christie as Lara. It was the first time we had seen love-making depicted so passionately on screen. As Lara rose from the bed, her face beaded with sweat, my friend and I looked at each other with horror. It was not the sex that had shocked us – it was the realisation that if you got so hot and sweaty during sex, your hair would go curly!

There was a brief reprieve during the sixties when wigs suddenly became a 'fun' fashion accessory. They were sold in department stores near the make-up counters as opposed to being hidden away in specialist shops. Wearing a wig was a witty fashion statement rather than an admission of the inadequacy of your own hair. It was magic. I could go out for an evening and never have to give the weather a second thought. Heat, rain, humidity, it didn't matter – my hair would remain as smooth and perfect as it had been when I left the house. It was quite addictive. And in the way that the high of drugs accentuates the down of real life, taking off the wig when I got home simply served to accentuate the forlorn state of my real hair.

Mary Quant arrived, and all the rules of fashion were being broken. Vidal Sassoon did a similar thing for hair. However one rule remained firmly in place: hair had to be straight. But then two things happened. First, the 1970s dawned, an era of long wavy tresses and afros. Second, a friend looked at my severely straightened hair and said simply: 'You know, your hair really doesn't look like you.' I looked in the mirror and suddenly saw that she was right. The severely straightened hairstyle didn't reflect the creative, quirky person I was at all. And that was the last time I straightened my hair. Who knows if I ever would have dared abandon my ironing tongs if not for the permissiveness of seventies' hair fashions?

I experimented with gels and potions and a thousand hairdressers who persisted in interpreting 'I want half an inch off' as: 'Cut as much as you want off – what the hell, who cares?' I finally found the right hairdresser and a carefully calibrated mix of gels, mousses and sprays that gave a bit of muscle to my fine curls. I thought I was finally set.

Fast forward twenty years to where I discover that, courtesy of a cancer diagnosis, I am about to lose all my hair to chemo. The initial panic – 'How will I deal with being bald?!' – didn't last long. To my surprise, I found I was relatively sanguine about it. After all, I'd had plenty of practice at disguising bad hair days and, in addition, I knew it wouldn't last forever. And I was right not to be concerned. Baldness wasn't nearly as bad as I had imagined it would be. In fact, it had some perks. I could just have a shower and dry my bald head with a towel. No potions or gels to firm up those curls; no time spent scrunch-drying under a slow and gentle heat to maintain those curls; no hairspray to make sure those curls didn't go floppy or limp. It really was like being that young tomboy all over again – I was back to wash and go. And, of course, it meant that I could wear wigs again. And this time, I didn't even feel as if I was cheating! I had a perfectly legitimate reason to wear a wig. I had one good wig that looked like my real hair (or, let's be honest, my hair on a very good hair day) and a couple of fun cheap ones. I relived the bliss of those earlier years when I could get dressed, put on my perfect hair and know that – rain, hail, sleet or shine – it would stay perfect.

Chemo ended. My eyebrows and eyelashes made shy appearances and my hair began to grow back. There was one window of time, when my hair was only slightly longer than a crew cut and I could comfortably leave the house without a wig or a hat. One summer day I was out for a walk in the heat when I started sweating. I headed to a nearby tap, turned on the cold water, dunked my head under it and walked away. It was exhilarating! Though not exhilarating enough to prevent me from growing my hair back to its normal length – just below my chin. It was as if that person with the wrong hair wasn't really me.

Soon my hair was back to looking as it had pre-chemo. Well, almost. It seemed to take more gel, more styling time, more everything to get it looking like my old hair. We forged a truce: I would put more time, product and effort into my hair, and it would grudgingly agree to resemble its old self. Once again, I thought I was set.

But it wasn't to be. I started to notice that my hair-gel consumption had increased. The curls that used to flop onto my forehead weren't flopping onto my forehead anymore. I couldn't work out where they'd gone. And then, one day, I caught sight of the back of my head in a mirror – and I saw scalp. At first, I was puzzled. Perhaps I had slept on it and really flattened that particular portion of my hair? Perhaps the hair gel and thickening mousse I was using weren't working anymore? (The infomercials did caution you to change your hair products every now and then so that familiarity didn't cause your hair to treat them with contempt.) Perhaps it was just grey roots I was seeing and mistaking for scalp? I looked more closely and then, with a shock greater than the one I'd received on accidentally viewing the critical scene in the film *Alien*, I realised what was happening. My hair was thinning. I was seeing scalp because – and when I looked closely

I could see this was occurring in many places – there was simply less hair and therefore more scalp on show. My curls were no longer dropping down past my eyebrows because my hairline had shifted, and in a bad direction. My hair gel was working just as well as ever, but there was less hair for it to work on. And, contrary to the claims on the bottle, it was not up to changing water into wine.

I zapped straight into thinning hair product mode. I bought everything. I tried everything. Hair-growing products, fibres that you dusted onto your scalp to simulate hair. Hair gels, mousses, shampoos, elixirs of every persuasion. Nothing really worked, but I found that if I spent a lot of time and used twice as many hair products as before, I could make myself look presentable. But every time I washed my hair, and before I'd thickened, dried, gelled and teased it, I could see it for what it was. What I saw when I looked in the mirror was the superimposed image of the little old lady who shuffles past you in the street, the sunlight lighting up her scalp beneath the sparse grey hair like the ominous Ghost of Christmas Yet to Come. What I was feeling was shame.

I was an intelligent woman with numerous accomplishments under her belt. I was smart, I was funny. I was a good friend and partner, a loving mother and a decent person. But none of that mattered when I saw my thinning hair in the mirror. I felt shame. And then I felt shame for feeling shame about such a ridiculous, external, trivial thing. I wasn't my hair. And yet, no matter how many times I told myself that, I discovered that some part of me thought I was.

I was also feeling bad about the amount of time I was spending on my hair. That was an easier one to solve.

I started listening to university lectures while I gelled, scrunched, dried and sprayed. The time itself became enjoyable and stimulating, but the feelings I had about my thinning hair were not so easily dealt with.

Thinning hair was very different from the straight/curly struggle. The curly hair of those years merely meant that you were unfashionable. Thin hair belonged to another animal altogether. It felt like the identification badge of the weak, feeble, inconsequential animal relegated to the back of the pack and soon to be discarded altogether.

It was one of the last hold-outs of the 'appearance-shaming' revolution. The fashion catwalks were starting to feature models of varying body shapes. Grey-haired women, beautiful and stylish, appeared in magazines as the 'face' of cosmetic or fashion brands. Older women were throwing off the label 'matronly' and wearing colourful, outrageous clothes and being feted for it. Women whose faces didn't fit the standard model for beauty were photographed for the top fashion magazines. All the old taboos were being discarded – except for one. There were no models on the catwalks or on the covers with visibly thinning hair. No-one whose scalp was showing. Oh, there were women who had shaved their heads, but that was different. That was a choice – a bold one that said, *I'm a strong woman.* Thinning hair, it seemed, said exactly the opposite.

My shame about my thinning hair didn't change. If I was out and realised that I had insufficiently disguised my hair problem – say, I'd caught a glimpse of myself reflected in a shop window and seen some scalp between the sparse strands – I would cringe internally. I started asking friends about their own 'bad hair days'.

Would they be as confident walking onstage to address an audience if they were having a bad hair day? To a woman, they all said no. These were all high-achieving professional women, yet each one of them had confessed they would feel less confident addressing a meeting, big or small, on a bad hair day. And each one of them said, 'I know it doesn't make sense, but . . .'

And there it was. Feeling bad about yourself because of your hair, or any other part of your appearance, doesn't make sense at all. And yet we do. And we persist in those feelings despite every logical part of our brain telling us we shouldn't. And that, of course, makes us feel worse. Not only are we feeling bad about our appearance, we are also feeling foolish and weak because we're feeling bad about our appearance – because, we tell ourselves, we don't have the internal fortitude or the relentlessly resilient psyche to truly follow that mantra of a book not being defined by its cover. We are punishing ourselves twice.

I knew all of that and yet it didn't matter. I still cringed when I caught sight of that scalp in public. I couldn't argue or intellectualise the feeling away. It felt beyond rationality. And perhaps it was. Evolutionary psychology is a field that looks at psychological traits and behaviours from the perspective of the most ancient humans. It looks for characteristics that may, in those times, have conferred a survival advantage and thus were innately valued. In many species, beauty is one of those survival-advantage characteristics. The bird with the longest tail feathers or the brightest plumage, for instance, is the one who snares a mate and thus ensure the survival of its genes. Each species has its own definition of beauty, and those characteristics are frequently at the top of the list of what it takes to win the best mate. It is thought that beauty, in its various permutations, signifies good health, vitality and an increased probability of healthy offspring, hence its evolutionary advantage.

In humans, many of the signifiers of beauty in women are also the signifiers of youth and health – dewy, unblemished skin, lush hair – and so, as with birds and animals, beauty, with its implications of robust fertility, signals good prospects for healthy children to perpetuate the line. This has led some evolutionary psychologists to believe that beauty in humans serves as a powerful signal, one which has been instinctively embedded in us since prehistoric times. This instinctive attraction to beauty is thus beyond the realms of reason and yet is understood by all. And so, by implication, those who fail to meet that standard may find themselves feeling 'less than' in a way that defies rational explanation.

I never got to find out whether I could have wrestled my feelings of 'less than' to the ground. A dermatologist waved the wand of a brand-new oral medication and, miracle of miracles, my hair grew back to an acceptable standard. I didn't have to find out what I was really made of. But in that long wrestle with my feelings, I did at least start to realise that I didn't have to feel so bad about feeling bad.

HOW COULD THIS HAPPEN TO ME?

We don't see things as they are, we see them as we are.

Anaïs Nin

Has there been a time in your life
when you discovered that things were
not as you assumed them to be?

My first husband left when our daughter was nine years old. I came home from work one day and found a note on the kitchen table that said: *Leave my books. I'll come back for them later. I've taken my clothes and I'm not coming back. Don't tell anyone. And by the way the power is off. Ring this number.*

I was shocked or, to be more accurate, I suffered from shock. I felt the physical pain of it. I couldn't think straight. I was a mess emotionally. I had no idea that there had been a problem brewing. What had I done wrong? Was I a bad wife? Was he having an affair? Had I not been paying him enough attention? I couldn't have been paying attention if he was so unhappy in the marriage he had to leave. Had I missed something? If I had, why didn't he say anything? Then again, communicating his problems didn't seem to be uppermost on his mind: he didn't just walk out of the marriage, he disappeared, as in completely vanished.

He was a journalist and a broadcaster. He had a PhD in astrophysics and was involved in an extensive education research project. He was passionate about science fiction and had built up a sci-fi club from scratch.

He was involved in political and social circles. But he walked out on it all: every job, project and club in which he was involved.

It was hard to get my head around. It wasn't as if he was an angry, arrogant male stomping around the house ranting when things didn't go his way. If he had been a boorish brute, I wouldn't have been surprised that he ended the marriage so brutally. But he was a gentleman: handsome, charming, funny, sensitive and well-read. Thus, when he left so abruptly, so brutally, I was devastated. Beyond devastated. It hit me with the force of a physical blow. I could hardly believe this had happened to me.

I had come from a family in which women not only worked, they were the equal of men. My mother was a mathematician who taught in a girls' school. She had gravitas. My mother could walk into a room and people would stop talking and turn to look at her. She was beautiful, smart and had a wicked sense of humour. She was compassionate and thoughtful, too. Whenever she gave advice, it was reasoned and sensible, and people listened.

My father was an architect. He loved books and read widely. When I was a child he read to me. His father, who had been a Hansard reporter for the early Australian federal parliament, had been a friend of C.J. Dennis, and my father would read the poet's verses aloud: '*Hey, there! Hoop-la! The circus is in town! Have you seen the elephant? Have you seen the clown?*'

We lived the life of the comfortable middle class. I was an only child and attended a private girls' school. I grew up in a household where a woman was expected to think for herself, so I was never reluctant to speak my mind.

My parents encouraged me to have my own opinions. When Elizabeth Bennet confesses in *Pride and Prejudice*, 'There is a stubbornness about me that can never bear to be frightened at the will of others. My courage always rises at every attempt to intimidate me,' I recognised those words. That was me: a contrarian by nature.

My parents loved me, I knew that, but they didn't think I was particularly bright. Unfortunately, I did not excel at those subjects they deemed to be academically significant, namely mathematics and the sciences. The things I was good at – writing and literature and art – were considered less important. While I grew up in a household filled with books, and books provided sustenance, wisdom, solace, delight and entertainment, in my parents' eyes they did not lead to a sustainable career. Nevertheless, when I won a scholarship to study literature at university my parents were delighted with my high academic achievement.

On graduation, my first teaching position was in a country town. I met my husband at the school there. He taught maths and science, while I taught English. We fell instantly in love. We had so many interests in common. Literature. Music. Books. Film. We shared a passionate interest in science fiction, which buzzed at the core of avant garde thinking in the 1960s, and read Arthur C. Clarke, Isaac Asimov and were particularly enthralled by the author Cordwainer Smith. This was the pen name used by the American intelligence officer Paul Myron Anthony Linebarger, who was based in Canberra at the time. He was an expert in psychological warfare and counterintelligence. His identity was not well known, so it was a coup to identify him; on our honeymoon we drove to Canberra to interview him for a science fiction magazine.

We were married in an ecumenical service. My family were Anglican. His Presbyterian. Then we quit our jobs and moved back to the city for what was intended to be a brief stay while we prepared to move to England. I dreamed of studying art at the Slade while my husband would write a sci-fi novel. Everything was going to plan until I fell pregnant.

We were all set to go. We had a farewell party. Yes! We were on our way. As we said our farewells and prepared to leave the party I got to the front door and froze. I was leaving on a grand adventure but I knew, as I stood immobilised at the front door, that I could not do it. Now that I was pregnant our plans had to change.

'I can't do this,' I told my husband. He just nodded.

We discussed our options and decided that he would go back to university and finish his PhD in astrophysics. Then, after the birth of the baby, I would return to work to support the family. We only had $300 in the bank; we had little choice.

It was at this point that I discovered his parents were not like mine. His parents were educated. They moved in the same social circle as my parents. They talked about books, music and art. But they were bound by propriety and duty. Afternoon teas in their sitting room were formal and tense. His mother cooked but there was no joy in serving food. Alcohol was never offered. There was one telling incident before we married, though I failed to pick up the cues at the time. My husband had bought me a diamond engagement ring. His mother bristled at the sight of it. It was, in her view, obscene, far too ostentatious. My future mother-in-law not only abhorred showy displays of wealth, luxury or intelligence, she was appalled by displays of exuberance or emotion. My husband grew up in a loveless home run by a dour, domineering mother.

When I announced that after the birth of the baby I would be going back to work to support her son as he finished his PhD, his mother said disapprovingly: 'If you go back to work, that child will grow up to be a delinquent and we will have nothing to do with you. We will disinherit you.'

I gave birth to a beautiful daughter. When my mother-in-law came to the hospital to inspect her first grandchild, I asked her if she would like to hold the baby.

She grimaced. 'I don't like children.'

'But you had four of them,' I said, aghast.

'We had to populate Australia,' she replied.

My mother-in-law never showed any fondness for her first grandchild and positively loathed everything I did as a mother. When I went back to work, she fumed. That was the man's job. You could read the disapproval in her tightly clasped hands and pursed lips. We didn't care. This was the late sixties. Society was undergoing a revolutionary change. However, what I wasn't able to recognise till much later was that my husband – raised as he was by a cold, controlling mother and a formal, often absent, father – had no idea how to be a parent. He did not understand the responsibilities. He tried. But there were occasions when he could not put his daughter's needs before his own.

At the time, we were living a bohemian life and saw ourselves as intellectuals. My husband was studying on a radical campus during the anti-Vietnam war protests. He was a member of the International Anarchists. I was, at the time, tutoring at the same university. He asked me to leave my job. 'It gets in my way,' he told me. I assumed being on staff made me a target, and at that stage no-one knew how violent the evolving protests and sit-ins would become. Violent student protests were erupting around the world. I thought my husband wanted to protect me in turbulent times, so I did as he wanted and quit. Later, I realised this hadn't been his reason at all. It was because I was a tutor and he a mere student. This upset his world-view. A wife cannot have a higher status than the husband.

I had a small baby to care for and I was teaching, but we were muddling through. When it was time to christen the baby, however, we ran into a major stumbling block. I wanted her christened in the Anglican Church, but my husband's family was Presbyterian. My husband approached the issue like an academic inquiry. He inter-viewed theologians for three weeks to authenticate the legitimacy of an Anglican christening, finally concluding that the Anglican Church was sufficiently Christian.

A week before the christening the Anglican minister visited me at home.

'I've just had a phone call from your mother-in-law,' he said. 'I've been told in no uncertain terms that I should not christen your daughter.'

I stared at him, speechless.

'Don't worry,' he reassured me. 'No-one tells me what to do in my church.'

We didn't see much of my in-laws after that. You might call it a blessing!

My husband finished his PhD and then moved into various avenues of employment, including broadcasting work, journalism and academic research. My mother was instrumental in securing him a research position through her contacts. Meanwhile, we maintained our interest in science fiction. My father had bought a small farm close to the city in the early seventies. My husband and I had great plans for this venue. We planned to restore the old farmhouse and run sci-fi conventions on weekends. And that's what we did.

The sci-fi fraternity at the time was indeed a fraternity. The convention participants consisted almost entirely of men aged 18 to 24. I enjoyed these 'nerdy' conventions, but I was more focused on my teaching career. I had been appointed senior mistress at a city high school, becoming the youngest person to hold the post in the state at the time. I did feel a little uneasy telling my students to think for themselves while forcing them to conform to a uniform dress code, but apart from this ethical glitch, I was good at the job.

So there we were: a busy, successful professional couple with a young daughter. Then one day I arrived home from work with our daughter, put the key in the lock and opened the front door. The place was a mess. Books had been pulled off the shelves, clothes were strewn every-where and the furniture had been upturned. It looked as if the house had been ransacked. At first I thought we had been burgled. Then I found the note on the kitchen table.

I felt so foolish. Our life had been predicated on the fact that we were clever. We thought we were so clever we didn't need to talk. Then he walked out. I had a full-time job and a young child. I kept thinking: 'How am I going to manage?' I was confused and angry and absolutely devastated. And, as my husband had indicated on the note, for some inexplicable reason the power was out in the house. I rang the number on the note. I recognised it as belonging to a member of the sci-fi club who I had known for some years. He came over to the house and sorted the power.

I showed him the note. I was a mess, but he was calm as he read the note then looked around as if assessing our situation and considering what could be done to improve it. This was not surprising; he was an engineer with a rational turn of mind.

'I'll be back tomorrow with a television set,' he announced. I was dubious. My husband and I were intellectuals who didn't watch TV; that's why we didn't own one. My champion pointed out that my daughter would need a distraction while I worked out what the hell was going on.

He was as good as his word. The next day he arrived with a brand-new TV. He set it up, turned to my daughter and said, 'There you are. Now you can watch anything you like.' Those were magic words for a TV-deprived nine-year-old. While my daughter sat mesmerised by the flickering screen, my champion helped me put the house back in order.

I still didn't know how I would cope as a single working mother. There was no after-school care in those days. The mothers' network helped me by taking my daughter to school in the mornings – something her father had done previously – and minding her when I had to attend evening meetings. They didn't ask prying questions. I was barely functioning, though. I was numb and broke. My husband and I had had a joint bank account, but he had cleaned it out. How could he do that? Half that money was mine! How could he leave me with no cash to get by until my next payday?

It was my year twelve class that snapped me back

to reality. After a week of me shuffling into class and mumbling a few inept instructions, one of the boys said to me: 'We don't know why you are unhappy and we don't need to know, but we do need to pass year twelve. So, if you don't mind, would you get on with teaching us?'

This was just the bucket of cold water I needed. It woke me up. And I realised that, in many ways, I was fortunate. I had married at 25. Now, at 36, I had a career, good standing in the community, a clever daughter and supportive parents. When my mother read my husband's letter, she snorted. 'Don't tell anyone?' she said, incredulous. 'That's ridiculous. You can't pretend nothing has happened. You have to get on with your life.'

My in-laws were true to form. When a friend told them that their son had left his wife, my mother-in-law replied: 'We've never thought much of her or that child. As far as we're concerned they don't exist.'

Even though I didn't want anything to do with my in-laws, this comment still wounded me at a time when I was vulnerable.

I asked a prominent academic who knew my in-laws for advice.

'My advice to you,' he said, 'is to remember that they're elderly. They'll be dead in ten years. Ignore them. Act as if they are already dead.'

This was much better advice than that proffered by my local vicar when I told him of my distress. He said: 'There's a ladies sewing circle making hassocks. You might like to join them.'

The vicar's wife, however, was much more pragmatic. 'You know I don't like to speak ill of other people, but don't listen to your mother-in-law – she's mad.'

My cousin, with whom I was very close as we had grown up next door to one another, gave me the most practical advice of all.

'Here's the name of a good lawyer,' she said. 'And don't take your husband back under any circumstances.'

On the surface, I managed to get my life back on track. I could function in the world. Go to work. Buy food. Care for my daughter. But inside I was dead. The end of my marriage was a spectacular and public humiliation. I couldn't feel anything except the crushing pain of shame. For the first time in my life I had not only experienced failure, I had no idea why I had failed.

It was my cousin who came to my rescue once again.

'Remember what we used to do when we were kids? The whole family would sit around the table discussing all sorts of problems, but the conversation was not over until we laughed.'

So that's what we did. My cousin and I talked and talked until it all looked so ridiculous that we couldn't help but laugh. And there was so much to laugh about. First, there was the inevitable flood of men thinking that I was available and in need of a man. Some of those encounters were frightening. One time the teenage boy next door chased off a man he saw loitering in my backyard at three in the morning. (I had lights installed after this incident.) It was obvious that many single men were simply looking for a 'little lady' to take care of the house – well, I wasn't 'little lady' material!

Then there was Oscar Wilde, whose work I'd loved since my parents enrolled me in acting classes when I was twelve. My cousin reconfigured many an Oscar Wilde quote to suit my circumstances.

'To lose one husband, Mrs Worthing, may be regarded as a misfortune; to lose one so completely looks like carelessness.' That gave me a big laugh.

After a year's absence, during which I had heard no word from him at all, my husband reappeared and asked me to take him back. I was astounded. As he stood at the front door asking – *expecting* – me to take him back, I realised that I had fallen out of love with him. The process of falling out of love is much slower than falling in love. It's not sudden. Rather, it's a slow unravelling, thread by thread. And then there was also the anger. That was not so easily forgotten. As William Blake put it, 'It is easier to forgive an enemy than to forgive a friend.'

Over the years that followed, I encouraged my daughter to have a relationship with her father, so we never lost touch completely. I can't say we were the best of friends, but we were polite to each other. I watched as he stumbled through multiple relationships and an assortment of jobs, but I said nothing; I knew it was not my place to criticise. Besides, I wanted us to stay on cordial terms for our daughter's sake.

It was only many years later that I found out why he had left. He was by this stage terminally ill. I visited him often as there was no-one else in his life other than our daughter, and in that time we became close friends again. Now, at last, I could ask the question: 'Why did you leave?'

The answer was unbelievably trite.

'The journal I submitted my research to refused to publish my paper. So I just decided to walk out on them. You were collateral damage.'

It took time and many discussions with a mutual friend to understand how the rejection of a research paper had led him to walking away from his marriage. In hindsight, the signs had been there all along. The problem was his ego, his fragile ego. On the outside, he was a success, all charm, wit and sensitivity, but on the inside his self-belief was as fragile as fine crystal. During our marriage, whenever his ego got in the road I just manoeuvred around it or acceded to his demands, such as when he ordered me to quit my tutoring job. But why was his ego so fragile? And why did the rejection of his research paper have such a huge impact on him? I came to the realisation that his problems had begun in his childhood. He was not loved as a child. As I've explained, his mother was cold and domineering and his father absent. And if you are not particularly loved by your parents, you must find your self-worth elsewhere, outside the family. So his sense of self-worth came from winning, from being the best at whatever he did. He won a scholarship to university. He was a debating champion. He was a prominent dissident at a time of unrest. He was an esteemed academic. A successful broadcaster. An astrophysicist in an era when astrophysicists were the rock stars of science. He had to win at all costs. If he did not win, he was nothing.

When I was promoted to a senior position in my profession, his ego was bruised. When our smart daughter started asking him questions he could not answer, he became annoyed and then defensive. He did not like to be challenged. The final straw was having his research paper rejected. He couldn't stomach the thought that maybe he wasn't better than others, that he wasn't smarter than everybody else after all.

When the journal refused to publish his research paper, he was so outraged by this slight to his ego, he stormed out of his life. This may not have been a good career move, because the rest of his life did not turn out as he would have liked. He couldn't hold down a steady job, but this was not an insurmountable problem; he was still handsome and charismatic and had no trouble finding women willing to support him. I was merely the first in a long line. Ironically, I was the only woman who stood by him up until his death, and after he died, I ended up with his ashes. So I did take him back in a way.

But by this time my attachment to him had diminished. I no longer felt the emotional pain that was triggered when he first walked out on me. When my husband resurfaced after a year away, and I discovered that I was no longer in love with him, I realised I could finally get my life in order. I asked him for a divorce. At last, I was an independent woman. I knew that I had successfully reclaimed my life when I attended a sci-fi club event one weekend and another club member made a passing observation. It was such a significant moment for me I can even remember what I was wearing: I had on a little black top, a short black cone skirt by an Italian designer embroidered with largish pink and purple tulips, and flat black shoes.

As I sashayed into the meeting, the club member – an older man – turned to me and said, 'So, Venus is rising again, I see.'

She was. But I was not alone. I was with the man who had been a great support through my troubled times. My champion, the engineer who my husband had told me to call to fix the power, had become my rock and my lover. And, reader, I married him.

SYNCHRONICITY

I am open to the guidance of synchronicity . . .

Dalai Lama

Synchronicity is an ever present reality for those who have eyes to see.

Carl Jung

The definition of synchronicity is 'a coincidence of events that appear to be meaningfully related but do not seem to be causally connected'. Have you experienced synchronicity in your life and, if so, what impact, large or small, has it had?

My mother had her babies young, between the ages of 22 and 28. There was no family history of difficult pregnancies and yet, from when I can first remember thinking of babies, I always felt instinctively that I would find it difficult to conceive. There was no objective reason for this. I had always been a strong, healthy girl and I grew into a strong, healthy woman. Nevertheless, the feeling was there.

Not long after we were married, my husband and I had the conversation about babies. I felt ready, my husband a little less so, and we agreed that there was no hurry. Two years later, when I was 32, we both felt that the time was right. I went to the doctor for a check-up to be sure I was in good health and ready to start. I was very organised about it – I wanted to do everything right. I worked in various managerial roles and was accustomed to dealing calmly and competently with crises, and I approached conception in the same way.

During our relationship, my husband and I had frequently had sex without using contraception. I'm not a wild risk-taker, yet somehow this never felt like a risk to me. It's odd when I think of that now. Had my body communicated something to me? Or was I perhaps unconsciously trying to prove it wrong?

At any rate, although I had had a fair amount of unprotected sex without falling pregnant, and despite the shadowy feeling that it might be difficult to conceive, another part of me still thought: how hard could it be? It seemed to me to be mostly a matter of getting your timing right, and that was something calculable.

The doctor's check-up proceeded flawlessly. Like a racer on the starting blocks, I had heard the starter's gun. I was off and running.

Except that I wasn't getting anywhere. Month after month my period arrived. Finally, I decided that it was time for some help – I needed the nudge of science.

I took myself off to the doctor's again. He sent me to a gynaecologist who specialised in fertility problems. The gynaecologist suggested that I start by taking Clomid to stimulate my ovaries into producing more eggs.

I was relieved, as this seemed like a relatively small intervention. So, for six months I took Clomid, and for six months nothing happened. Of course, when I say that nothing happened, plenty happened – it just wasn't what I wanted. Each month, my hopes rose, and each month they plummeted. Each month I told myself that this would be it, this one would do the trick. And each month, my body told me that it wouldn't. Finally, I decided I had to be realistic: my body needed more than the nudge of Clomid. I gave in and went back to the doctor for the big guns – IVF.

People told me that IVF could take time and repeated efforts to work. 'Yes, yes,' I said, 'I understand.' But, really, I was sure it would work the first time. In my mind, it was like exchanging ordinary steering in a car for power steering. How could it not work?

I started IVF – and it was a game-changer. Yes, it's true that when you're trying for a baby and sex is regulated by the calendar, it's not the free, impulsive love-making of the past. It's freighted with things that weigh a lot more than sexual desire. But it's still just you and your lover – two people alone in a room, intimate and private. Once you begin IVF, however, you stop being a person and become part of a science experiment.

On the outside, I was a 'good' patient. I was compliant, conscientious and courteous. I understood that the procedures I had to undergo were part of the science, and the science was clinical, detached, objective – numbers, biochemical interactions, scans and procedures.

Inside, of course, there was nothing clinical, detached or objective about my experience. I was a human being, not a science experiment, and my feelings oscillated between hope and disappointment. The overwhelming emotion I felt during the IVF treatments was frustration. I knew in theory that the process of fertilisation and pregnancy required numerous moving parts that all had to be perfectly synchronised. But at the same time, it felt as though it should be a simple, natural process. Women got pregnant all the time without even trying. What was wrong with me? And why was even science finding it difficult? I was doing everything right and it still wasn't happening.

IVF involves a number of steps. First come the stimulating drugs, designed to prod the follicles into producing eggs. Then, after a certain number of days, there is a scan to see which follicles show signs of producing eggs.

The eggs are harvested while you are under a general anaesthetic. You then go home and wait for a call to tell you how many eggs have been collected.

Once the eggs are collected, the next step is fertilisation. If you are using your partner's sperm, he has to provide it to order. Then there's another phone call to tell you how many eggs they've fertilised. Then it's time for the transfer.

I found the transfer process very strange. I lay on a couch with my legs up in stirrups, holding my husband's hand. The embryologist came in holding the embryos in a pipette. I couldn't take my eyes off it. Was my baby in there? As the specialist went about his work, the procedure was projected onto a screen. I could see it all happening. It was impossible not to be excited. The whole process was about putting everything in the right place at precisely the right time and it was happening before my eyes. Of course it had to work. How could it not? This was science!

Ten days after the transplant, I returned to the clinic for a hormone test which would tell us whether the embryo had taken. There were no grey areas here – it was either on or it was off. After the test, I had to go home and wait out the day in suspense until they called to tell me which it was.

Friends and professionals have plenty of suggestions to help you cope with the waiting. None of them work. Your whole body knows you are waiting. Your soul knows you are waiting. It is not possible to forget.

Finally, the phone call came. It was a no.

After the crush of disappointment, I gave myself the pep talk. Okay, I said to myself, everyone told me that it might not happen the first time and they were right. That's okay, it's bound to happen the second time.

Many women produce enough eggs on their first go-around that they don't have to repeat the whole process but can go straight to fertilisation and implanting when the time is right. I wasn't one of those women. I had to go through the entire procedure again. And I was met with the same devastating news as before. The implantation had failed.

I repeated the process a third time, a fourth time . . . all the way through to a ninth time. The result was always the same. Finally, the specialist told me my eggs were of poor quality and that's why the implantations were failing. He didn't think it was worth continuing; it was unlikely to produce a different result.

The breath left my body.

'You could use an egg donor,' the specialist suggested.

'How do you do that?' I asked.

'It's not easy,' he replied.

And he wasn't kidding. It is very, very hard. In Australia, unlike some other countries, it is illegal to pay egg donors. You are allowed to pay the donor's medical expenses but apart from that no money can change hands. Some women do donate eggs – they are called egg angels – but there are very few of them and there are very many of us: the women desperately seeking a donor egg. My husband and I started to explore where and how you advertise for an egg angel, but we were fully aware of how slim the odds were of finding one. And then, just as we were about to begin the search, something amazing happened.

Not long after the specialist's appointment, I was talking on the phone to a dear friend of mine. I have known her since we shared a house twenty years ago. We were strangers who happened to land in the same place by the sheer chance of apartment and housemate transactions, and we forged a connection that was closer than that of many sisters. We had each moved around in the years since, but we always maintained our connection. When each of us married, we met each other's husbands and the bond between us continued to deepen. We felt like family to each other. My friend, who now had four children, had been with me through every stage of my journey to conceive and had shared my pain with each hopes-raised, hopes-dashed failure. I was telling her about our research into egg donation, explaining that we were about to begin the search for an egg angel, when she said, 'I want to donate my eggs to you.'

I was shocked into speechlessness, doing goldfish impersonations on the other end of the line as I tried to get my voice to work. Not that I knew what to say. I was in a state beyond words. How many people in the world are ever offered a gift of this magnitude? It was almost confronting to experience generosity on a scale like this.

'Are you sure?' I asked, when I finally recovered the ability to speak.

'I've thought a lot about it. I've had my children. I know what you've been going through. I want you to have a baby nearly as much as you want it. If I can help make that happen, then I want to do it.'

While I was still reeling, overcome by this miracle of a gift, she continued, 'I know myself. When those eggs leave my body, they will be yours. It feels like a blood transfusion to me. Once your blood is taken and infused into someone else, it becomes a part of them. It becomes their blood. That's how I feel about my eggs and giving them to you.'

When my husband heard of the offer, he was as over-come as I had been. But he had more doubts.

'Wouldn't it be better to get the eggs from a stranger?' he said. 'It's straightforward that way. You don't have to deal with the extra emotional issues that a gift like this can raise. It could be difficult having the eggs of someone we know.'

I could understand where he was coming from, but I knew my friend well enough to be certain that there were no strings attached to this gift. And though I would feel grateful for the rest of my life, I knew that my friend was not offering this gift with any expectation that it would need to be 'paid back'. It was genuine and carefully considered. Her husband, she assured me, was as keen as she was to offer us this extraordinary gift.

'Wouldn't it be better to have the eggs come from someone we both know and love?' I countered. On reflec-tion, my husband agreed that it was.

So it was decided. And once decided, it felt so totally right and perfect to all of us.

I told my doctor the momentous news. He responded that a donation of this nature was taken very seriously by the clinic – both couples would have to see a counsellor, and the two families would be appraised to ensure that everyone understood the emotional ramifications of what we were proposing to do.

We were taken through all the 'what if' and 'what happens when' questions: What happens if you change your mind? What happens if you find yourself wanting to be more than an egg donor? What do you tell the child as he or she grows up? What do you tell the four children you already have? When do you tell? And how do you tell?

However, the interviews with the counsellor were surprisingly easy. We were so secure in our deep friendship, in our knowledge of each other and in our love for each other, that it had always felt like a soul friendship. And who else would you trust to always wish the best for you and to be there to do whatever they can, freely and generously, other than a soulmate? The four of us and our friends' four children already saw ourselves as family and this new baby would be part of that family. My husband and I would be the mother and father and my friend would be his godmother. They would know each other as 'family' from the beginning and, as time went on, the story I would tell him about the egg given to me by his godmother would become more complex and realistic as his ability to understand grew. When my child was old enough to understand the story, my friend would then tell her children about her donation. We were in synch emotionally with every question the counsellor asked, and it reinforced for all of us the sense of 'rightness' about this venture. In the face of a barrage of scientific tests, impersonal doctors and coldly clinical procedures, this felt like the most natural part of the whole process.

Once the clinic had determined that we were in synch emotionally, we then had to be synched on a physiological level. My friend's ovaries were stimulated to produce eggs while I took hormones to suppress my cycle so that when the eggs from my friend had been fertilised and were ready to be implanted, I would be in the right part of my cycle.

And it happened. For the first time in all these years, I fell pregnant! It was thrilling to finally get the phone call that said 'yes!' instead of 'no'. We were all beyond excited. It felt like magic. I was 38 by this time – six long years into my attempt to conceive. I had always thought there would be a child in my life before I turned 40, and now we were heading for the New Year and I would meet it pregnant. I would have a baby by the time I reached that borderline marker in my mind.

That New Year's Eve was one of the best of my life. The traditional wishes for the New Year – may it be bountiful, fruitful, full of joy – precisely echoed my inner being. That was what I felt: bountiful, fruitful, full of joy. I went to sleep that night knowing that I was going to wake on the first day of a year full of all the promise and new life I had wished for.

I woke at 5 am – bleeding.

I was six weeks pregnant and I was miscarrying. And suddenly I was Cinderella caught after midnight – all the magic had turned to ashes in a tick of the clock. I would start the New Year in sorrow instead of joy.

I was distraught. My eggs were not good enough but, by a miracle, we had overcome that. But it seemed I still could not sustain a pregnancy. Did this mean that, not only were my eggs inferior, my body itself was not good enough?

At the clinic following my miscarriage, I cornered a nurse. I was desperate. 'Isn't there anything else I can do?' I pleaded. 'Anything else at all I can try?'

The nurse hesitated. 'It's controversial,' she said, 'and not everyone agrees with it, but there's a book that you could read. It's called: *Is Your Body Baby Friendly?*'

I located that book at the speed of light. It was sub-titled *Unexplained infertility, miscarriage and IVF failure explained* and was written by fertility specialist Dr Alan E. Beer. I recognised myself on every page. Dr Beer theorises that some women's immune system goes into overdrive when they get pregnant and that the 'natural killer cells', the soldiers of the immune system, attack the embryo, believing that it is a foreign object. He believes that treating the immune system of such women so that it doesn't attack the embryo would allow them to have a full-term pregnancy.

I made an appointment with my specialist as soon as I finished the book.

'Tell me about natural killer cells,' I said.

He sighed. 'That theory hasn't been proven,' he replied. 'I won't work with it.'

Okay, I thought to myself, then I'll find someone who does.

I did some research and found two specialists who believed in the method. The first one that I met hit the right mark with me. He was a no-bullshit kind of doctor. He didn't make any promises, but he did say that if I wanted to try this treatment he would be happy to take me on as his patient. 'It's an invasive procedure,' he told me, 'and I use a methodology that's different from many others. If you want to come on this journey, then this is the science behind it.' And he explained the medical reasoning on the immune system and infertility. He was straightforward: the statistics weren't on my side, he warned, but we would see what we could do.

At around the same time that I had my first consultation with the new specialist, a friend told me that she had heard of a clinical psychologist with an excellent reputation who, as well as being a psychotherapist, was also a hypnotherapist. 'Why don't you go see her?' she suggested. By this stage, I was open to trying anything that might help, so I made an appointment.

I had never been to a psychotherapist before, let alone a hypnotherapist, and I was unsure what to expect. But the connection between us was immediate and felt absolutely right. As I told her my story, the questions the psychotherapist asked and the observations she made assured me that she really understood what I was going through. As a result, I felt safe to talk openly about my feelings: the fear, the hope, the anxiety, the stress, the weight on my heart – all the complex emotions this journey had aroused. I didn't have to put on the calm, competent, matter-of-fact mask I wore in my dealings with the medical profession and visits to the clinic. I could just be me. It felt so good to be fully recognised and accepted.

When I had finished telling my story – which was not just the story of my IVF experiences but the story of the relationships, family and life experiences that had shaped the person I was today – my therapist laid out a plan. She suggested we book a number of weekly sessions while I was in these crucial stages of the IVF process. We would use those sessions to talk about what was happening for me emotionally but also, importantly, to do some hypnotherapy aimed at maximising the success of the IVF procedure as well as helping me to cope with the stress. We would begin the hypnotherapy the following week and she would record the session so that I could play my hypnosis recording regularly between our meetings. She went on to explain the process of hypnotherapy to me, to dispel any myths I might have heard.

Many people have the mistaken belief that hypnotherapy is an airy-fairy New Age technique that has no scientific basis. In fact, I learned, there is an extensive body of scientific research to support the efficacy of hypnosis. Rigorously tested laboratory and clinical results have been published in peer-reviewed medical journals worldwide.

One of the other big myths about hypnosis is that it involves someone taking control of your mind. In fact, it is the opposite. In this setting, the therapist is teaching you how to use your unconscious mind to access inner resources that have previously been unavailable to you. In effect, the therapist is teaching you how to gain greater control of, and access to, your own mind. Some of these resources are psychological, such as the ability to feel relaxed when you would otherwise be tense, the ability to feel confident when you would otherwise be anxious, the ability to see situations with greater clarity and to feel more in control.

As well as offering you access to these inner psychological strengths, hypnotic suggestions can also shift some physiological systems in a positive direction. For instance, hypnosis can be used to affect the vascular system; that is, hypnotic suggestions can often stop or minimise bleeding. Hypnosis can speed up recovery from surgery. It is helpful for minimising the side effects of cancer treatments, such as reducing nausea and vomiting. Essentially, it can be used as a tool to help the body maximise its healing ability. Not everyone can achieve these effects, but many can.

Most people have only heard of a connection between hypnosis and pregnancy in the context of pain relief during childbirth. However, the immune system has been shown to be responsive to hypnotic suggestion, as has the endocrine system – the system which modulates the secretion of hormones. The endocrine system and the immune system are both involved in IVF treatment and, in addition, hypnotherapy also lowers stress, which in turn helps the body function better. One study a few years ago concluded that hypnotherapy significantly increased the chances of success with IVF. My therapist told me she thought we had a good chance of optimising my body's response to the treatment.

This first session felt like a turning point in what has been a long and bumpy road. I felt as if I was finally on the right path.

In the next session, we began the hypnotherapy, and I loved it straight away. It made me feel calm, clear and grounded. It was like taking a deep breath in the middle of a storm – therapeutic and strengthening. In the following sessions, we continued to talk and also to use hypno-therapy to work with my body. We focused on the womb, on the hormones needed and the immune system, which had to be made to protect the embryo rather than attack it. These sessions were wonderful – even wondrous. For years, my body had belonged not to me but to the doctors, to the clinics, to the impersonal demands of science. Now I was able to reconnect with my body. To work with it lovingly instead of resenting it. To have a sense of 'speaking' with it rather than feeling estranged from it. In a time of disempowerment and fragmentation, my therapy sessions kept me feeling whole. They renewed my confidence in myself.

Meanwhile, the time for implanting the embryo had arrived. I was on the new drug regime recommended by my specialist. I was excited, optimistic. And when the half-dreaded, half-anticipated phone call came days after the implantation, I learned that I was pregnant. I was overjoyed. My husband was a little more cautious than me, adopting a wait-and-see approach. He had learned to fear being too optimistic.

A few weeks went by. My work had always been busy and demanding, but those demands had suddenly escalated. We were understaffed – one staff member was overseas and another was on leave – at a time when crucial deadlines were suddenly imposed on projects for which I had primary responsibility. Each minute was spent working against the clock, finding ways to mitigate the stresses and workloads of the people who worked under me, reassuring clients and trying to produce the best work possible in what felt like the atmosphere of a hurricane. As a senior manager, it was important that I appeared calm and in control, and I felt as if I was succeeding in that.

One Friday evening, we were out at a restaurant. After an extremely stressful week at work, it was good to be able to relax. I felt conscious of my good fortune. The new IVF method was working, I was pregnant, there was so very much to be grateful for. Suddenly, I felt blood starting to flow. In that first instant, I fought against the awareness, desperate to believe that the sensation was something else, anything else. But I couldn't ignore the reality. We scrambled to leave. My husband paid the bill while I went outside to hail a taxi and ring my gynaecologist to tell him I was having a miscarriage.

I was devastated. In the weeks that followed, I struggled to free myself from the despair I was feeling. I'd had so much faith that I was on the right path at last. I didn't know how to get back up again.

My therapist guided me through the grief. And she also made an interesting observation. Although I had thought I was keeping my cool in the pressure-cooker of work, she wondered whether my body had been absorbing the stress in place of my mind. I didn't know for sure whether this was the case, but it rang true.

This was knowledge we could use, my therapist assured me. And she included in the hypnotherapy some suggestions that there was a stress buffer around my body. No matter what stresses I might experience at work or at home, my body would be protected from them.

I felt the difference almost instantly. Work continued to be demanding – there were competing deadlines, I still had to juggle a number of different projects and clients while under-resourced – but now I had the sense that I was insulated from those stresses.

It was a couple of months before I felt ready to try the IVF again. There was only one embryo left, which meant that this would be my last chance. That knowledge was terrifying – after all these years, everything rested on this one cycle.

When I next saw my specialist, I asked a foolish question. Embryos are graded according to their 'quality'. Grade A is best, B not as good and C inferior. What grade was my one remaining embryo, I wanted to know.

'C,' my specialist replied.

I was crushed. That meant the embryo had a relatively low chance of healthy survival in the uterus after implantation.

My therapist and I talked about this and what it meant: how one could both accept a grading while at the same time realising that it could not predict the future; it was only an estimate. Some grade A embryos will not implant and some grade C's will grow to become healthy babies. Nothing was set in stone. Right now, the future was still wide open.

We talked of how difficult it was to maintain hope in the face of failure or overwhelming odds. How even hoping, in these circumstances, could feel dangerous – and yet it was all that kept us going. We thought about the process of renewal. Of how to move on. It was like the difference between a maze and a labyrinth, my therapist told me. A maze has many dead ends and multiple choices of paths. As you walk through a maze, it is impossible to know if you are on the right path or on a path that leads nowhere. You are forced to make constant choices, as paths branch off frequently, but because you have no overview you have to make those choices blind. There are many wrong choices to be made in a maze and many ways of becoming stuck.

A labyrinth, by contrast, has only one path. There are, therefore, no choices to be made. The path winds around and around towards the centre and then unwinds again. The exit point is the same as the entrance point. However, because the labyrinth is a tool for meditation and self-discovery, if you have walked the labyrinth in that spirit, you will not be the same person when you exit as the one you were when you entered. You will be walking through the same physical space but occupying a different emotional space.

You have only one task in a labyrinth: to attend to each step as you take it and to be fully present as you walk. You cannot see what lies ahead as the path constantly curves. You have only the present; the future is unseen.

You must trust the path. The labyrinth is an ancient symbol for wholeness. It represents a journey into the centre of ourselves and back out into the world. My therapist said that she thought I was walking through a labyrinth.

It felt instantly right. And the analogy was deeply calming. At that moment, there was only one path. I could not see ahead and my task was to walk that path one step at a time, bringing to each step as much of my whole self as I could. The image of the labyrinth would come to my mind many times after that session, and each time it brought with it a sense of inner stillness, of being deeply centred.

And so, I approached the next, and final, IVF procedure. The odds were against me. I was already forty years old by this time. There was only one embryo left and that embryo was a C grade, but it was all I had. There would be no more after this. It was my last chance.

I used the self-hypnosis techniques my therapist had taught me as I readied myself for the implantation process. And then I waited. Finally, the phone call came – I was pregnant!

One week went by, two weeks, three, four, five. I felt wonderful. We hadn't told anyone yet about the pregnancy – I was carrying this amazing secret around with me, our own private piece of bliss. In the sixth week I had to take an overnight trip to Sydney for work. I arrived in the morning, went to various meetings, and then returned to my hotel room for a good night's sleep before my flight home the next day.

I woke in the morning to find the bed covered in blood. The shock was as great as if I had woken next to a dead body. I called my specialist back in Melbourne. 'Get back here as soon as you can and come straight to hospital,' he said. I thought frantically about how to manage this. I called a friend and asked her to ring the hotel and get them to send up some sanitary napkins so that I could at least walk from the room without leaving a trail of blood. I was in a cold sweat – I couldn't believe this was happening.

I emailed my therapist to explain the situation and asked if she could fit me in for a session when I got back to Melbourne.

Just a few minutes after I'd sent the email, my phone rang. It was my therapist. 'Do you want to see if we can try to stop the bleeding with hypnosis?' she asked.

I understood the subtext of her question. We had talked about the fact that sometimes miscarriages happen because the pregnancy is not viable. But this pregnancy felt right. I had nothing except my intuition to guide me, but I was sure of it. Yes, I told her. I wanted to stop the bleeding.

'Okay', she said. 'Lie down on the bed with the phone near your ear. We're going to do some hypnosis over the phone.'

And that's what we did. She guided me into the hypnotic trance state and through images and suggestions of the bleeding slowing and then stopping. Then she woke me up. I felt calm, connected to my body again, no longer overwhelmed by the out-of-control feeling the bleeding had inspired. The flow of blood had reduced to a trickle. When I left the room a short time later, I was no longer bleeding at all. But I still didn't know if it was too late. There had been so much blood. I was terrified that I had lost the baby.

My husband met me at the airport and we went straight to the ultrasound clinic. We held our breath as the gel was applied and the ultrasound wand moved over my belly. I was expecting to see nothing – no baby, just emptiness. Then the ultrasound technician said, 'Can you see that little pulse?'

We peered at the screen. Yes, we could see it.

'That's your baby's heart,' she said.

I rang my father, a doctor, to tell him the news. 'Isn't it amazing?' I cried.

His response was guarded. 'Let's just take it one day at a time,' he said.

My husband, too, was cautious. We had been here before, after all. He no longer dared to be optimistic.

The weeks turned into months. I started to look visibly pregnant and then *very* visibly pregnant. I was entering the third trimester now – the home run. At 28 weeks pregnant I was feeling good. More than good – I was feeling safe. The anxieties of those first few weeks were behind me. This was really going to happen.

We were having a quiet Saturday night at home. I got up to go to the bathroom and suddenly there was a gush of blood. I was overcome by pure terror. In the car ride to the hospital, I was in shock – I couldn't believe this was happening.

I was still bleeding heavily when we reached the hospital. The doctors were worried. My specialist told me that we might not be able to prevent the baby's very premature birth.

As the bleeding continued, my specialist ordered an ambulance to take me to another hospital, one with a specialist neonatal unit. If the baby was born so soon, he or she would need specialist treatment for many weeks. I was pale with fright and shaking like a leaf – I knew all the risks involved. I couldn't bear to think of my baby sick or fighting for life.

The ambulance arrived and I was carried out on a stretcher. My mind was racing. I couldn't be having the baby now. It wasn't right. I felt as if I had lost touch with my body. I had my phone with me, so I emailed my therapist and explained what was happening. It was 10 pm by now, so I didn't expect a reply, but I hoped she might check her messages in the morning.

To my surprise, a text came back almost immediately. 'I am ten minutes away from home,' it said. 'I will ring you when I get there.'

And sure enough, ten minutes later my phone rang. 'Ask the ambulance driver if you have five minutes before you get to your destination,' my therapist said.

I checked with the driver. 'Yes,' I told my therapist. 'I do.'

'Then we're going to do some hypnosis,' she told me. And she guided me into trance and into suggestions for stopping the bleeding.

We arrived at the hospital seconds after she had woken me up. One of the paramedics who'd been accompanying me came around to help me out of the vehicle and into a wheelchair.

When she saw me, she looked startled. 'What just happened?' she asked. 'You look like a different person from the one we picked up. You look so calm.'

I was wheeled out of the ambulance to the hospital entrance only to find that it was closed due to the lateness of the hour. The paramedics had to wheel me around the whole hospital perimeter before finally finding an open door. It was like a scene in a bad sitcom. But through it all I remained completely calm. I was back in touch with my body. And I could feel that the flow of blood had slowed dramatically. By the time I was admitted into the hospital, it had subsided.

My specialist wanted to keep me in hospital for a week in case the bleeding recurred. My therapist, who was in Sydney for a conference, called each day and we did some hypnosis over the phone. She also told me the story of that night.

She was at a workshop which was supposed to end at 11 pm. Because of her flight to Sydney the next morning, she decided to leave an hour early. She was in the car with the radio on when she realised she had left something behind at the workshop venue. She pulled over to text a friend who was still there to pick it up for her. Within seconds, there was a reply to her text. Except, as it turned out, it wasn't a reply to her text, it was my email from the ambulance coming through. If my therapist had stayed at the workshop, she wouldn't have heard the incoming ping. If she hadn't forgotten something and pulled over at the exact moment that she did, the car radio would have drowned out the ping and she wouldn't have seen my message until the following morning. And if the ambulance had been just two minutes closer to its destination when she rang, we wouldn't have been able to do the hypnosis. It was one of those rare moments when the universe is exquisitely aligned. Two minutes either way and it wouldn't have happened.

The bleeding didn't recur and I left hospital at the end of that week. The rest of the pregnancy was uneventful.

At 38 weeks I went into hospital and gave birth to a beautiful healthy boy who got full marks on the AGPAR, the newborn health score.

My wonderful little boy has just turned three and I love being his mother. Before he came along, if you had asked me, I would have said that there was something missing in my life. Now, after giving birth to him, I would rephrase that. What I have discovered is that it was not something missing in my life – it was something missing in me: the part of me that was meant to be a mother but did not have a place to surface. Since my son's arrival, what I now feel is an extraordinary wholeness, like nothing I have felt before. I feel complete.

GIVING AND RECEIVING

'Tis better to give than to receive.

What gift, that you have either given or received, has had an impact on your life?

In January 1995 two things happened almost simultaneously. The occurrences weren't related (though they had a deep underlying connection) and neither were they out of the ordinary, yet they would prove to have profound consequences. The first was that my mother went to see a movie with some friends. The second was that I read a book.

My mother regularly went to the movies with her friends – she enjoyed seeing films and chatting about them afterwards over coffee and cakes. There was only one type of film she absolutely refused to see: those set in the Second World War. So when she met her friends in the cinema foyer that fateful afternoon and discovered that the film they had arranged to see was *Schindler's List* – Steven Spielberg's film about the Holocaust – it was only her natural politeness and consideration for her friends that prevented her from walking straight out again. Instead, she watched the film.

At around the same time, I settled down to read a book that had been sitting on my shelf for a few weeks. Written by psychiatrist Paul Valent, it was titled *Child Survivors of the Holocaust* and comprised a series of interviews with Holocaust survivors who had been children at the time. They had been hidden, disguised, sent away or given away. Hardly any Jewish children came out of a concentration camp alive – children, the elderly and pregnant women were routinely sent straight to the gas chambers upon arrival. Only 6 to 11 per cent of Jewish children in Nazi-occupied territory survived the war.

My mother was born in Warsaw in 1939. It was not an auspicious time to be born. Nor was it an auspicious place to be born. And it was a particularly horrifying time and place to be born if you were Jewish, which she was. When the Warsaw Ghetto was established by the German authorities at the end of 1940, all the Jewish citizens of the city were ordered to leave their homes and relocate. The ghetto was then closed to the outside world. Leaving the ghetto was punishable by death and any person who knowingly helped shelter a Jew faced a similar fate. Overcrowding in the ghetto was extreme; there were, on average, eight to ten people per room. That's per *room*, not per house. The residents were allowed to bring very few possessions with them, and the authorities severely limited food supplies. The lack of medical care resulted in outbreaks of infectious diseases. These and other privations led to a soaring death rate. Then, in 1942, the Nazis began the mass deportation of the Warsaw Ghetto Jews to the extermination camp of Treblinka.

For some years before the war, my mother's family had employed an elderly, non-Jewish nanny to look after my mother's brother, who was eight years older. On being moved to the ghetto, my mother's parents, believing that their baby would not survive the ghetto, made the heart-wrenching decision that in order to save her, they would have to give her to the nanny to care for.

Taking the baby was an act of great courage on the nanny's part; she was literally risking her life for my mother. I can only speculate as to her motivation. Was it her attachment to the family? Her love for the baby? Her horror and repugnance at what the Nazi regime was doing? It could have been any one of these reasons. We'll never know.

The nanny took my mother to live with her in the country, concealing the baby's true origins. But such a pretence was dangerous, and more than once – whenever the nanny sensed that her neighbours' suspicions had become aroused – my mother would be sent elsewhere for a time.

My mother's brother, meanwhile, stayed in the ghetto with his parents. During one round-up, when Jews were to be herded into trains heading for the death camps, his mother grabbed him and hid with him in the toilets and managed to evade deportation. When word spread that another round-up was imminent, my uncle fled the ghetto. Fortunately, he was blond-haired and blue-eyed; at first glance he appeared Aryan rather than Jewish. But he was circumcised, which would instantly betray his heritage if anyone were to discover it. With nowhere to go, he lived on the streets, where he not only had to contend with the threat of discovery but with the possibility of starvation and hypothermia too.

My mother's aunt – her father's sister – had left for Russia when the war broke out. She begged her daughter, who was married and had a baby my mother's age, to accompany her. However, her daughter's husband refused to leave his parents behind in Poland, and so my great-aunt's daughter and grandchild stayed behind with him. My mother's aunt returned to Poland after the war to find that almost all of her family, including her daughter, grandchild, son-in-law, her son-in-law's parents, her brother and her sister-in-law (my grandmother and grandfather), had died at the hands of the Nazis. There was some good news, though: her brother's children, my mother and her brother, had survived. My great-aunt wanted to take them to Australia, a country of safety and freedom. But my mother's brother, who was fourteen by this time, refused to go. He wanted to stay in Poland, which was now under Soviet rule. Having been hunted and reviled, he longed to live in a society in which everyone was equal, and he saw the embodiment of this dream in communism.

And so, at the age of six, my mother moved to Melbourne, Australia. Her aunt adopted her and became her mother. After some years, my uncle, disillusioned with life in the communist state, followed her to Australia, though he ended up settling in Sydney. Deeply scarred by his wartime experiences, he became a virtual recluse. I only met him on a couple of occasions when I was growing up.

My mother spoke very little about her experiences during the war – it was clearly a painful subject. Understanding that talking about the past was excruciating for her, and not wanting to distress her, I refrained from asking questions. I knew only the barest of details: that she had been hidden as a baby and had thus survived the genocide. I had friends whose parents had been teenagers or young adults during the war and had been subject to the horrors of concentration camps; I was grateful that at least my mother had been spared that. But it was not until I read *Child Survivors of the Holocaust* that my eyes were truly opened to the experience of child survivors, and it was life-changing.

Reading the interviews, I understood for the first time the trauma experienced by these children who had been separated from their parents. I was a young parent myself at the time, and that understanding was sharpened by my own experience of mothering young children. I believe it was the shock of this realisation that gave me the impetus to ask my mother directly about her wartime experiences.

At the same time, seeing *Schindler's List* had unlocked something in my mother. Through some magic of synchronicity, she was ready to talk just as I was ready to listen. And when she did talk, my mother made a request that startled me. 'I want you to find my uncle,' she said. She believed an uncle of hers had survived the war and was living in America. This was why, she explained now, she had always loved everything American. She had given her daughters names that were typically American, was devoted to American movies and TV shows and had a keen interest in all aspects of American culture. In this way, she felt she was maintaining a connection with her long-lost uncle. However, even though she had known of her uncle's existence since her teens, it was only now that she was in her fifties that she felt ready to look for him.

She could only provide me with scant details with which to begin the search: a surname which might or might not have changed, and no first name – and this was in the days before the internet. I wondered if my uncle, my mother's brother, might have more details. I contacted him and we arranged to meet. It was the first time I had seen him in fifteen years. My uncle, though a highly intelligent man, was very wary of people. He had retained his wartime fear that, as a Jew, he might be persecuted. He even anglicised his name on arrival in Australia. He had never married or had children. Like my mother, he was reluctant to talk about the past. Nevertheless, he agreed to share with me what little he knew about his uncle. My uncle thought that he might have been in the diamond business, and that it was also possible he was residing in Israel or South Africa.

And so I began my search, with only a surname (which might have changed), a possible profession and a search area that encompassed a large part of the globe. International phone calls were exorbitantly expensive in those days, and the line often crackled with static. Faxes were the only other means of reasonably speedy communication. I contacted the International Red Cross, which was helping to reunite family members. They put ads in various newspapers for me. I also put my own ads in multiple newspapers in the different countries. The Mormons, with their huge genealogy files, were helpful and gave me lists of names to pore over. I managed to obtain the passenger arrival lists for Ellis Island, the immigration station for those entering the United States through New York during the years in which my great-uncle might have emigrated. I contacted guilds of diamond merchants for lists of members' names. Streams of names, dates and details poured from my fax machine. By six months into the search, I had acquired thousands of names, details and professions – and almost all irrelevant. But somewhere within that staggering mass of data, there might just be the one name or detail that would lead to my great-uncle.

Weeks and then months went by with no leads, not even false ones. I was almost cross-eyed with exhaustion. Finally, I decided it was time to admit that the task was impossible. I decided to give up. But then, only a few days later, my mother asked with a hopeful smile, 'Are you getting anywhere?' I went back to the data.

Close to seven months into my search, some details clicked: the right name, the right time of emigration. It was him! I had done it! I felt a buzz of excitement imagining my mother's response when I told her I had at last found her uncle. Hastily, I faxed for more details. 'I remember my sister had a club foot,' the reply came back. My hopes were dashed. My mother's mother had not had a club foot.

I went back to the data once more. By this time, I was growing apprehensive – my mother's hopes had been raised. What if I couldn't deliver? It would be devastating for her.

More months passed. The Red Cross rang and told me that, while they would keep the file open, it was no longer active. They were discontinuing their search. I begged them to run one last ad, and they agreed.

I was not optimistic. After all, we had run so many ads, in so many places. Made so many phone calls, sent so many faxes, pored over hundreds of lists of thousands of names. After a year, all this searching had produced nothing. What could one last solitary ad do?

As it turned out, it could do a lot. My great-uncle's son saw the ad. The family had changed their surname, but everything else fitted. His father had passed away some years earlier, but his son knew enough to fill in the details. We found that there were two first cousins we had never known about. And I found another cousin, too, living in Belgium, and she was able to remember my mother's parents. We organised a family reunion for the end of that year: we would all meet for the first time in Hawaii.

Before the reunion, my mother's cousin in Belgium sent us a photo from before the war. A family of 25 was posed in front of a beautiful gazebo. My grandmother looked exactly like my mother and my grandfather looked exactly like her brother.

It was the first time my mother had seen her parents. 'How do you feel?' I asked her.

I didn't really need to ask the question; the look on her face said everything.

'You have given me the greatest gift,' she said. 'You have given me my family.'

She had given me a gift, too. I felt immensely grateful that I had been able to do this for my mother.

That gift extended to my uncle, who had moved back to Melbourne; my search proved the catalyst that brought him back into the family fold. From then on, he came to Friday night dinners and was present for all family occasions. Being a cherished part of the family was a source of great joy to him for the twenty years until his death. When he was terminally ill, we were able to care for him, helping with his doctor's visits, his hospitalisation, his medical bills and other practical affairs. We all visited him regularly and together ensured that, when he died, he knew that he was loved and valued.

Nearly three decades after I'd found my mother's family, my youngest daughter went to Poland with a youth group. One evening, the organiser emailed to tell me that the group would be going to visit the Children's Forest in southern Poland, a site that commemorates Jewish children murdered during the Holocaust. 'You might like to send your daughter a note to read out loud on her visit to the forest,' the organiser suggested. I had three hours to think about what to write.

My darling daughter,

It must be very emotional to be where you are. I can't imagine.

Although I am far away in Melbourne, I too am very emotional writing this letter picturing you over there. You are now standing in a forest somewhere in Poland where your nana and great-uncle were born. Nana's parents were sent from the Warsaw Ghetto to an extermination camp and were murdered along with many other family members: cousins, aunts, uncles and children. In fact, Nana's aunt, who adopted Nana after the war, had a granddaughter the same age as Nana. She was only three or four when she was murdered.

And now you are here, a grown child, a teenager, standing in the Children's Forest in Poland. Nana's parents would be so pleased to know that your nana and your uncle survived. They would be especially relieved to know that, in handing their precious baby daughter to her nanny, they had made the right decision. They would be so pleased and proud to know that Nana married your Zaida and had two children and seven grandchildren and that you, the youngest grandchild, would one day visit Poland to honour their memory. Please say a prayer on

*my behalf, and on behalf of your grandmother
and great-uncle, to convey love and respect to all
our family and all the Jews who perished and were
murdered in such a horrific way.*

*Dad and I are very proud of all that you have
achieved in your eighteen years already, and your
great-grandparents would be too.*

Love,
Mum and Dad

JUMPING TO CONCLUSIONS

As you think, so you become . . . Our busy minds are forever jumping to conclusions, manufacturing and interpreting signs that aren't there.

Epictetus

What conclusions have you jumped to, walked up to, or taken on without even realising? And how have these conclusions affected your life?

I was in my forties and had just changed careers. I was at a conference, feeling like a total outsider, which was an oddly familiar feeling – it was like the first day of a new school when I changed mid-term. I was the odd girl out: the only one who didn't know the routines, the classrooms, the teachers or any of the other students. Further ahead of me in the queue to register, I noticed a woman dressed in a striking outfit. People were constantly approaching to greet her. She was just like one of the popular girls at school, the ones I had always wanted to be like.

After the morning tea, we were separated into small discussion groups. The striking woman was in my group. To my surprise, when I put forward my views on the topic we had been assigned, she immediately spoke out in support of my position. When the session ended, she asked me if I wanted to grab some lunch with her. I presumed she meant the lunch provided by the conference, but she had other ideas. 'You don't want to eat the dried-up sandwiches they've provided,' she said, 'and I can't be bothered talking to the others. Let's just sneak off to the cafe around the corner.'

We stayed at that cafe talking for so long that we were late getting back to the conference. We stole into the back of the lecture theatre. A rather boring man was droning on and my new friend scrawled some hysterical comments about him on her notepad and pushed it over to me. We were both shaking with silent laughter, to the point where other people were turning to look at us, clearly wondering what was going on.

We discovered we lived quite close to each other and were both at a similar stage of life – partnered, with children old enough to take public transport to school and jobs that allowed us a lot of flexibility. We fell into the habit of meeting up for coffee at least three times a week, and in between those meetings we'd have long phone conversations about anything and everything.

We grew so close, so quickly, it was as if our friendship was meant to be. We didn't tend to go out as foursomes with our partners – it was more fun with just the two of us. We had our own in-jokes, we practically had our own language. It was like being in an exclusive club.

Often, when we were at a cafe, other women would come up to greet my friend. A lot of people seemed to know her – and, more than that, they seemed eager for her friendship. She'd be scrupulously polite to their faces, but as soon as they left, she'd make such scathingly witty assessments of them that I'd be reduced to laughter.

On one occasion, her phone rang. She looked at it, made a face, but took the call. Whoever was on the other end of the line was obviously wanting to arrange a date to meet up. My friend came up with a variety of excuses for the different dates proposed. She was sounding perfectly friendly, but all the while she was making 'get me out of here' faces at me. Finally, she extricated herself from the call. 'Some people just can't take a hint,' she said. I looked at her questioningly. She shrugged. 'We used to be close friends,' she said, 'but I've moved on and she just doesn't get it.'

I'd had good friends at school, but I'd never had a 'best' friend. My family moved often due to the demands of my father's job, so I was always starting new schools. Inevitably, just when I'd started to make friends, we'd have to move again and I'd have to start all over again at a new school.

I always found the first weeks at a new school nerve-racking. Everyone had their friendship groups settled already and they weren't looking for new additions. Usually, the few people who were looking for friends were those who had been rejected by their peers. If you partnered with them, you were sealing your position at the bottom of the social ladder.

Some kids can flourish as the 'new kid' because they're charismatic or glamorous or have a killer sense of humour. They become a prized commodity – people want to have them in their friendship groups. I had none of those char-acteristics and yet at each new school I still had to try to 'sell' myself, fully aware that I was trying to hawk goods that even I recognised were department-store quality rather than boutique. I was eternally amenable, going along with whatever the group thought, being helpful whenever I could, adopting the language and ethos of my new friends. It was the only way I knew to be accepted and, as a teenage girl, acceptance was everything.

Given all the practice I had, as new school followed new school, I grew to be reasonably good at it. I was always part of a group, but at the same time, I was always conscious of having to be on my best behaviour; I was always on probation. Equally, I never had a best friend – there was never the time to develop that kind of relationship.

The new friendship that bloomed from that conference felt like the realisation of all my old schoolgirl fantasies about the best friend who totally 'got you', who was always there for you. I couldn't believe my luck at finally stumbling across a platonic soul mate. I think I was high on it.

My new friend was the kind of person who would have been tagged 'high social status' even at kindergarten. She had a kind of social magnetism that drew people to her and she radiated confidence. With no fear of exclusion, she said exactly what she thought. I marvelled at her freedom to do that. And, very slowly, I began to allow myself to do that too.

Once, instead of automatically agreeing to meet at the cafe she had chosen, I suggested a different one. She wrinkled her nose – that place had terrible coffee, she said. Another time, my car was out of action, which meant I couldn't get to the place where we had planned to go for a walk. I hoped she would suggest picking me up or perhaps a change of meeting place. Instead, she suggested we put it off until the next week. I shrugged off the slight feeling of disappointment – it was nothing – and our friendship continued in its usual pattern.

Eleven months had gone by and the conference at which we'd initially met was coming up again. My friend had been swamped by work lately, so we hadn't been able to catch up as much as usual, but we were going to share a ride to the conference and I was looking forward to it. I rang her to check what time she wanted to be picked up.

'It's a bummer,' she said, 'but I have to drop in some-where else on the way to the conference, so I'll take my own car in.' I was about to offer to drive her anyway – I didn't mind a detour – when she said, 'Oops, there goes the doorbell. Have to run! See you at the conference.'

I found myself feeling unreasonably dejected that we wouldn't be arriving at the conference together after all. Get a grip! I told myself. It was hardly a catastrophe; we'd still have plenty of time to catch up.

But when I looked for her at lunchtime on the first day of the conference, I couldn't find her. I texted her, but no reply came back. I started to worry. Maybe some-thing had happened? I kept an eye out for her but she didn't appear.

When the lectures resumed that afternoon, I sat myself at the back, near the door, so that I'd see her when she walked in. By the time the second session was about to begin, she still hadn't turned up. I was about to text her again, sure that some emergency at home had called her away, when the door to the lecture theatre opened. In walked my friend, deep in conversation with another woman. She walked right past my seat and didn't even see me. I had a sudden flashback. 'Some people just can't take a hint,' I heard my friend saying all those months ago. And I knew in that moment that it was my turn to be 'some people'.

It was devastating. I called her many times, trying to organise a meeting so we could at least talk things over. But each time there was some excuse. Finally, I stopped calling. I cried in a way I hadn't cried for years. I kept thinking about her, trying to work out if it was something I'd said or done, but since she refused to meet me I never did get any answers. It took months for me to get over it. It was as painful as any romantic break-up I'd ever had – I felt as if I were in mourning for something I would never get back.

In the aftermath of that break-up, I felt all kinds of emotions: hurt; sadness; anger directed both at her and at myself; confusion at the unfinished nature of it; and shame, too, at being rejected. At the same time, I had a sense that I shouldn't be feeling so intensely about what was 'just' a friendship. My friends felt that too. It was as if it was legitimate to feel distressed after a romantic break-up, but not after a friendship break-up. And yet, in any close relationship, whether it is with a friend or a lover, we offer up a part of ourselves to the other and trust that it will be valued and kept safe. The emotions we feel if that trust is broken are essentially the same.

My distress faded eventually, and I could at last think about what happened without a sense of heartbreak and shame. And when I observed our friendship from a distance, I saw that the clues to its demise had been there from the start.

The friendship had always been conducted on her terms. We met where she wanted to meet and when she wanted to meet. I had been willing to fall in with her plans – I was accustomed to doing that from my school days. Fitting in with others felt like second nature to me. And perhaps because it was so familiar, I barely noticed it and it didn't bother me. I learned from that friendship that I should notice it, and that if all the fitting-in was on the other's terms and for no good reason, it should bother me. It should have been a sign that she considered her needs to be more important than mine.

The other clue was much more obvious – and I had noticed it, though I wilfully ignored it. Over the course of our friendship, I was being presented with conflicting messages. On the one hand, I was being told how special our friendship was, how different from the others I was and how much she cherished me and always would. On the other hand, I was witnessing her treatment of other people, including ex-friends: the sarcastic put-downs behind their backs, the politeness in public and the denigration in private. I saw her treat people with contempt, as if they were disposable objects, while at the same time accepting her implicit assurance that I was different – a treasured and valued friend.

I couldn't believe both messages simultaneously, so I jumped to the conclusion that I wished were true: that our friendship was special to her, that I was different from those other people she laughed at and that our friendship was real and lasting. She would never treat me like those other people.

From the vantage point of some years later, it seems clear that the rational approach would have been to watch how she treated others and to know that sooner or later I was going to be treated like that myself. That was simply who she was. I leaped to the conclusion I did partly because she was so convincing in her protestations of eternal friendship but also because of my own needs. Who doesn't want to find their soul-mate friend? Who doesn't respond to being told they're special? Who doesn't want a dream to come true? And who hasn't avoided the truth staring them in the face because they'd really rather not know?

THE SHORT SHRIFT

There is but one cause of human failure. And that is man's lack of faith in his true Self.
William James, American philosopher, 1842–1910

**Have you at any time had a lack
of faith in your true self?**

When I was four years old, the local butcher leaned over the counter in his soiled white apron and asked me, 'What's your name, little girl?'

I was outraged. 'I'm big!' I snapped, glaring up at the large man. But I wasn't big. I was already short and slight for my age then, and my height and weight would always be well below the norm.

My family lived in Bedford, New York, on a four-acre property. I was the third in a family of five children, but the only girl. My parents had met during the Second World War and hardly knew each other when they married. It was not a happy union. My mother, a bright and capable woman, found herself married to an obstinate man – one who saw himself as a successful businessman but who had no business sense at all. My father ran a heating and plumbing business in an area where the post-war housing boom was in full swing. The business should have been successful. It wasn't. Money was always an issue in our house.

The donkeys arrived in my life when I was seven years old. A client of my father was struggling financially and unable to pay his bill, so he offered my father two donkeys instead. My father brought them home in his plumbing truck. We had plenty of room on our property; there was a corral big enough for the donkeys and a shed to house them in winter. But my father had not really thought through the burdens of donkey ownership. Donkeys cost money. They eat food. There are vet bills. Their hooves have to be cut back annually. They need vaccinations. My mother thought my father had been a fool to take them, that they were nothing but a waste of money. She hated those donkeys. But I loved Jennie and Minnie. I loved them with an intensity I'd never known before. I loved them even more than I loved my parents.

I have to admit, though, that they were not lovable creatures; whenever I tried to ride them, they would bite and buck. But they were my friends. And they got used to me. When I would stand beside them and feel their warmth, when they nuzzled up to me, I felt loved. And their braying, a sound which drove my mother to distraction, was a welcome sound to me. It was just their way of saying hello.

Before long, the care of the donkeys fell to me, despite the fact that I was only seven. I had to fork the hay into their corral, using a full-sized pitchfork that was almost taller than me. I had to fetch buckets of water to fill their trough; those metal buckets were so heavy it took all my strength just to lift them and I had to carry them with two hands. I would also take Jennie and Minnie out each day to stake them on some grassy verge where they could graze, then bring them back home at night. They always resisted being led; every day it was a battle of wills. In winter I had to hammer a stake into often frozen ground with a full-sized sledgehammer. In summer I had to spray them with repellent to keep the flies off. But I did it all without complaint. The fact that I struggled to complete each of these tasks because I was so small confirmed in my mind that I was incompetent. It never occurred to me that my brothers were bigger than me or that I was simply too young for the responsibility.

It didn't help that Jennie and Minnie really were trouble. Sometimes they escaped and ended up in neighbours' gardens eating their prize roses or pulling washing off the line. The neighbours would complain and I would have to go and round up the errant donkeys. One time they chased a neighbour's dog into their pool. The dog nearly drowned and the neighbours were furious. So was my mother. I felt small and helpless and overwhelmed trying to stand up to a strong woman and stubborn donkeys.

I had a recurring dream in which I'd failed to feed the donkeys. I'd forget I had donkeys, then I'd suddenly remember I hadn't fed them. Terrified, I'd run to the corral to fork their hay over the fence, but when I arrived they were already dead of starvation. This dream continued on into my adult life. I constantly worried that the donkeys would die of hunger. This was ironic, considering that I was so small as a child that the doctor feared for my health; I was 'failing to thrive', apparently.

I loved those donkeys for more than eight years. Or, rather, I loved Minnie for that long. Jennie died after four years. I felt such loss and pain it physically hurt, but far from being sorry my mother just got angry. The donkey had to be buried, but it was winter, which meant my parents had to pay for an excavator to come and dig a hole in the frozen ground. Jennie was buried in a nearby pine forest. For years I would visit her grave and mourn for her. It was such an eerie setting. In summer, I'd crunch over the carpet of pine needles on the forest floor until I came to a brown needle-carpeted mound. This was Jennie's grave. And I would stand there thinking of the stubborn, bucking, nipping donkey that I'd loved and feel a knot of pain in my heart. But I didn't cry. 'Only babies cry,' my brothers said.

Because I struggled to perform my chores when caring for the donkeys, I'd always assumed that my small size made me incompetent, and this was reinforced as I got older. My height often marked me out as different from my peers. This was especially the case in my teenage years. When I started high school I became even more self-conscious. My mother didn't believe in making the best of your looks. She did not approve of fashion trends or make-up. While the other girls matured and began to dress to suit their new figures, my mother was still buying my clothes in the children's department. I struggled to keep up in class, too. I was bored by my subjects and didn't put in much effort, so my academic record was nothing to brag about. Sport was another area in which I failed to excel. I was a little kid trying to keep up with the big kids. Basically, I felt inadequate on every level.

When I was fifteen years old, my parents packed up the family and moved not just to another state, but to another country: New Zealand. They had made this dramatic decision because there were four boys in the family and young men were being conscripted to fight in the Vietnam War. I was forced to give Minnie away. Despite my brothers teasing, I cried bitter tears when she was driven off in the back of a truck. I couldn't help myself.

The anger I felt towards my parents was indescribable. I didn't talk to them for an entire year. I seethed with bitter, hate-filled rage. But they didn't even notice, preoccupied as they were by all the work the move entailed – not to mention the anguish of farewelling everyone and everything we knew. In those days, long-distance phone calls cost a lot of money; money we couldn't afford. And aeroplane fares were expensive, so it was unlikely we'd ever return to visit our friends and family. Meanwhile, at the other end of our long voyage by ship, there were new schools to be sorted, jobs to be found. Through it all, I grieved for Minnie. My parents dismissed my sullenness as typical of a teenage girl.

Moving to New Zealand had one enormous advantage for me. My brothers and I were sent to the local high school, and it happened to be a very good one. The teachers cared about and encouraged their students. I blossomed in this environment. I applied myself to my studies and my marks improved dramatically. And not only was I achieving academically, I found I could conquer physical challenges too, if I picked my mark. I was the only girl on a biology excursion to climb to the top of a mountain. For the first time, I realised that I did not have to be held back by my size. I became a driven and competitive student; proving that I was competent meant everything to me.

My high grades took me to university. I was in the first batch of students to study primary school teaching at a tertiary level. We were smart, and cocky too. We were going to be the best classroom teachers ever. At university, I became politicised and joined the protests against the Springboks' tour of New Zealand during the Apartheid era. I joined the throng shouting, 'Shame! Shame! Shame!' It was exhilarating for me to be a part of a movement. More and more I was realising that my size was irrelevant; it was my actions that counted. I even found a boyfriend – who would later become my husband – at these protests.

My first teaching job was very rewarding. The New Zealand system had high standards. There was a belief in discipline, and teaching was a highly respected profession. I had the freedom to innovate within the curriculum and be creative in the classroom. I believed that good teaching involved finding ways to help struggling students. One student, Peter, was a problem kid. I made sure to praise him at every opportunity, even if for trivial things. 'Peter,' I'd enthuse, 'you have the most highly polished shoes in the whole school.' For some students, even a modicum of praise made them feel they'd won a gold medal, they got so little of it at home. Being deprived of praise was something I understood well.

Another little girl had no friends. I soon realised that the other children were repelled because she smelled of urine. The school nurse and I organised a home visit. We spoke to her parents and discussed some ways in which they could help their daughter to overcome her bedwetting. Once the problem was solved, the girl's life changed for the better. There were many stories like this, and it made the job of teaching so worthwhile. I might have been small, but I was making a big difference.

Ironically, considering I married a New Zealander, I ended up back in America when my husband was transferred for his work. We were sent to the Midwest – Milwaukee – and I had to start my career all over again. To get into the teaching profession, you had to start with relief teaching, and all the relief positions were in the underprivileged areas in the inner city. The kids at the school I was sent to were tough – and big. Some of the year six boys were the size of adults. Suddenly I was painfully aware of my diminutive size once more, and all my old feelings of incompetence returned.

I can remember so clearly how intimidated I felt on my first day, as I looked up at the formidable three-storey brick building surrounded by concrete playgrounds and enclosed by a high fence. It looked like a prison. I watched the 'oversized' kids pushing and shoving each other as they jostled their way in the front gate.

I was given a quick induction by a senior teacher who basically said, 'We don't expect you to teach these kids anything. Your job is just to keep them in the room.' It was a horror scenario. There were no textbooks to speak of, no routine, and no respect for teachers. I walked into my first classroom and no-one even noticed me. There were kids hanging out the window and spitting on students in the playground below. Worried that one of them might fall, I told them to move away from the window. They ignored me. Some kids brought ghetto-blasters into the classroom, so I had to struggle to be heard over loud music and laughter. The students weren't necessarily bad; they were just totally disengaged. My presence didn't even register on their radar. I'd seek out a few of the interested-looking girls and try to teach them. It was all I could do.

I taught at four more schools, but I faced similar problems at each one. It was humiliating. I couldn't cope. My image of myself as a competent teacher was in tatters. I felt completely powerless. I was seven years old again and unable to manage the task I had been set. In the end, I gave up.

When, eventually, my husband and I moved again – this time to Sydney – I was determined to get another teaching job and prove to myself once and for all that I could do it, that I was a competent teacher. Again, the only jobs available were in the underprivileged areas, where the schools were considered to be rough. My first teaching assignment was at a school in the western suburbs. Relief teaching is never an easy job, as students always take advantage of the new teacher. I also discovered, leafing through the pages of the students' exercise books and finding most of them blank, that some of the regular classroom teachers did very little educating.

Towards the end of the school year, when students are always a bit ratty, I was assigned to teach a year six class for several weeks straight. These students would shortly be sitting tests to determine which high school they would attend. You wouldn't guess it from their behaviour, however. On my first morning, the students entered the classroom swearing and wrestling with one another. Even getting them to sit down was a major enterprise; one kid would pull another student's chair backwards so that he fell to the floor. Another was throwing books around the room. I have a deep respect for books and their impor-tance in education. Seeing them treated like this made me furious. I told the boy off. Far from being chastened, he just sniggered and whispered something to his mates. They all laughed. My hackles rose. I'd had enough. I would take a tough stance with the students from day one, I decided. I was prepared, organised and determined. I was going to teach these students. I might have felt powerless, but power came from caring, I believed. It would cut through the indifference.

I explained to the class that I wasn't there to babysit; I was there to teach them. They had tests coming up, and I knew I could help each and every one of them to get a good mark.

One of the students snorted in disbelief. I asked him what he got on his last maths test. He refused to answer, but one of the other kids called out: 'He got F for Fool.'

'I can change that,' I told him.

I knew if I could hold their attention, I could help them learn, and I would do this by making their lessons interesting.

'We've got a lot of work to do, but it's important we have a little fun on the way,' I told them. 'So we'll start each day with a joke. Who has a joke for me?'

It was probably some hideously unfunny fart joke, but they liked it. And from that moment, I had them.

I worked up a series of lesson plans that were both relevant and fun. We made Lego cars and raced them to learn about ramp angles. We made paper planes and threw them to learn about units of length. Relief teachers were usually dull, so I made sure I was animated, and always ready to listen when the students had something to say. My confidence in my teaching ability returned.

Watching the class transform also gave me a greater understanding of my own childhood. My parents had had no idea what a child might think or how a child may feel. We were fed, clothed and housed, but a child needs emotional nourishment too, even if they can't express that need. As I came to understand my childhood, I also developed an understanding of my parents. My mother was trapped in a life she didn't want but was powerless to change, and that had made her angry all the time.

My father, too, felt trapped. Preoccupied by the tensions in their marriage, they had little emotional energy to spare for their children. This was why they had never shown me any love and had paid me very little attention. As a result, I had felt small – and I could see now that this was not just a matter of my physical size. My sense of powerlessness and inadequacy had arisen because my parents had placed unreasonable demands on me – demands I struggled to fulfil – without even thinking about what that might do to my self-esteem. They were completely oblivious.

It made me sad to look back on my loveless childhood – but then I realised I hadn't been completely starved of affection. Two members of my family loved me. They just happened to be donkeys!

BEING KNOWN

He who knows others is wise; he who knows himself is enlightened.

Lao Tzu

Do you feel 'known' by the person or people closest to you, or are there parts of yourself that are unknown or held back?

It was July in Paris. The city of lovers had been the city of my fantasies since I was a young girl. In my imagination, I would wander its streets, wide-eyed and dazzled on my honeymoon or I would sip coffee in a small dark cafe with my new, passionate lover. There was always a man in my imaginings, even if his face and name were still hidden from me – Paris needed a man. I learned French as a schoolgirl and from the time I first heard its breathy, husky consonants and those vowels, so stretchy and sensuous that they melted into its rhythms, I knew it was the language of love, the language of seduction and romance. And I knew that one day I would go to the country where it was spoken.

And so, it was July in Paris. I was 48 and this was my first visit to the city. Indeed, it was the first trip overseas I had taken on my own. The marriage I'd imagined for myself was very different from the one real life had in store. The real-life marriage had ended in separation nearly three years earlier, but it had truly ended long before that. I had obligations, people for whom I had to stay, but I always knew I would leave – it was just a matter of waiting until the time was right. And then, finally, it was.

And so, I had not come to Paris mourning a lost relationship. I mourned that relationship while I was still in it. Leaving had meant freedom. Release from being someone I was not. I'd never pictured coming to Paris alone or so much older, but I was glad to be here, glad that I had made it happen. And being on my own was okay.

I was only here for five days, and I had a list of the usual touristy things to see and do – the Eiffel Tower, Montmartre, the Moulin Rouge – but more compelling than any of these was the luxury of simply wandering, letting Paris seep into my skin.

It was evening, around the middle of my stay, and I was out walking, dreamily absorbing the sights and sounds of Paris streetlife, when someone approached me.

He was an older man – at least ten years older than me – and he looked it, with his grey moustache, thinning grey hair, age spots and wrinkles.

'Are you in Paris alone?' he asked.

I nodded. I am someone who talks to strangers – I chat to everyone and anyone, and I have never been afraid to walk the streets at night.

He made a sad expression. 'You shouldn't be alone in Paris.'

I smiled. Or maybe I nodded. Whichever it was, I agreed with him. Paris was not supposed to be for the single.

He reached for his wallet. Was he going to take out money? But no, he was taking out a photo. People carry so many different kinds of photos in their wallets – photos of a spouse, a child, a sibling, grandchildren, beloved pets, a yacht, a mansion, a holiday. This was not a photo of any of those.

He pointed to it. 'This,' he said, 'is me. Myself.' He tapped his chest, just above the heart. 'Myself,' he said again.

We studied the photo together.

It was obviously him, but much, much younger. He stood with the confident swagger of a young man. His hair was thick and black, his skin unmarked. He was a very good-looking young man and everything about him – his stance, his smile – suggested that he was a real charmer. I looked from the photo back to him. The smile was the only thing that had remained.

'I live just over there', he said, pointing to a lit window in a nearby block of apartments. 'It is small, but it is better to live in a small place in the middle of Paris than a large place away from Paris.' He looked into my eyes. 'Come with me,' he said, and repeated: 'You shouldn't be alone in Paris.'

And I went.

His apartment was tiny. The whole of it could have fit in one room of my apartment back home, and my apartment is not considered excessively spacious. There was a bed, a miniscule bathroom and kitchen. The furniture was minimal. Apart from any aesthetic or financial considerations, there was simply no room for it. There was barely any room for us.

The sex was pedestrian – businesslike and quick. There was no talk, not even small talk. We were strangers. I kept the image of the photo in my mind throughout.

Afterwards, he offered me the use of his shower, but I declined. I wanted to get away from this grotty little apartment and back to my hotel room – a palace by comparison – and use my own shower.

I didn't think much about the encounter afterwards. It wasn't a bad experience and it wasn't a good experience; it was just an experience. It was what I wanted – an adventure. The sex was the least important part of it.

As a child and teenager, I had been quiet and rule-abiding at home. I was never offered emotional or spiritual guidance by my parents. They never asked about my emotional life. I felt loved, but to them parenting meant providing the basics: food, shelter, clothing, schooling. I don't think they knew how to do anything else.

All my parents saw at home was the quiet girl who kept to herself and didn't cause trouble. Outside the home, however, was a different matter. I brought myself up, and my primers were Enid Blyton books – *The Famous Five, The Secret Seven, The Five Find-Outers and Dog.* I devoured her books and her fictional protagonists became my role models. They were brave and adventurous. They went where they weren't supposed to go. They took risks. They got grubby and tore their clothes. They defied authority. And they weren't afraid. These were my real role models. I became a rule breaker and a risk taker. I wasn't quiet. And I didn't conform. My friends were always in the fringe groups; I could never understand people who kowtowed to the in-group in order to be accepted.

My Paris experience, then, was for the adventurer in me – the part that had responded to the derring-do antics of my childhood literary models. I didn't tell anyone about what I had done. Not because I was ashamed or embarrassed – I was neither of those – but simply because in my family we didn't share our experiences, not even with each other. I grew up in a house of secrets.

My mother sailed on the last ship from Poland before the war. She was sixteen years old. The rest of her family had remained in Poland, and all of them were murdered. My father was sent by his family to England to escape the Nazis. The British interned him and sent him to Australia on a ship called the *HMT Dunera*, which would later become notorious for the mistreatment of the detainees, including the young Jewish refugees who were sent to a prisoner-of-war camp in Hay, New South Wales. Like my mother, my father was the only one of his family to escape Europe. He too was the sole survivor of his family. Neither of my parents talked about their war and pre-war experiences in any detail, but my older siblings and I grew up knowing that they both had suffered intense pain and loss and had witnessed almost unbearable cruelty.

I was much younger than my older siblings; I almost felt like an only child.

At the dinner table, my brothers and sisters talked. They were older and louder than I was. If I chimed in, I was either ignored or told to be quiet. I became used to being the listener, the observer. Perhaps because of this, I also became the keeper of secrets. When my mother was 42, she unexpectedly fell pregnant. In those days, women of that age didn't have children – they were considered too old. My mother was deeply embarrassed by her pregnancy. She refused to tell anyone and disguised her condition in loose clothing. She didn't drive and would walk to her doctor's appointments in the evening. She wanted someone to walk with her and I filled that role, which was how I came to learn of her condition. I was ten years old and, for nearly seven months, I kept that secret from everyone, including my family and my closest friends. About three weeks before the expected birth date, my mother called the family into the living room and announced that she was pregnant. That was the first they knew of it.

Despite their remoteness, my parents had clear favourites among their children. My father loved the firstborn, a girl, because he had lost a sister in the Dachau concentration camp. The next child was a boy – the only son – and he and my mother were close. Then came a sister who was also close to Mum. And finally there was me, and I was a daddy's girl. And yet despite these connections, I'm not sure that my parents really knew any of their children. They knew what they looked like, of course, and what they achieved in school and so on, but they didn't know who they were inside. They didn't know what they thought, felt, feared, loved or hoped for. Emotional issues were never mentioned, let alone discussed. There was a matter-of-factness to everything and no curiosity as to why someone might feel or think one thing or another. We were brought up to adopt that same matter-of-factness, a kind of businesslike approach to life: 'It happened, it's over, move on.' Everything was external and nothing was internal. I never thought about my life – my inner life, that is – until I was in my sixties and I went to my first salon.

My family's attitude is, of course, the opposite of the salon approach, where we think about our inner lives, explore them, unearth our stories. When I went to my first salon, I was startled by the idea of meditating on the patterns and discoveries of one's own life. It was as strange to me as if the sun had turned purple. And I loved it.

The salon gave me permission to explore myself for the first time in a safe environment. When I told various stories about my life, I got feedback and a different perspective. I was quite stunned by some of the reactions. There are things I've done that seemed very ordinary to me, but to some people they were amazing, brave and even, some said, inspiring. I was astonished when they said that. Hearing those responses helped me to grow and see different parts of myself and recognise the strengths I have.

Listening to other people's stories has also helped me grow. Hearing how they have responded to their own life experiences has helped me to sort out my own issues, given me a different appreciation of how my mind works. And it has been fascinating to see how people with different backgrounds, belief systems and philosophies approach the same topic.

Sometimes, when you're listening to other people's stories about how they have dealt with various obstacles and difficulties in their lives, you think: Wow, that was impressive. And then you realise that you've also managed to deal with something like that. You can recognise parts of yourself in other people's experiences and it allows you to see yourself from a different perspective.

It's a process that brings your strengths to the foreground – it frees you up. And everyone is open about their mistakes. There's a recognition within the group that we're all human; we don't judge each other. I learned more about myself – who I was and who I had been – in the first three salons than I had learned in my whole life.

When I got engaged, my mother said to me, 'You're getting married and I don't even know you.' I said, 'Yes.' She wasn't wistful. She didn't say it regretfully. It was just a statement of fact. And I responded equally matter-of-factly – she was right; she didn't know me. I look back on that moment now and it strikes me that at least she was aware that she didn't know me. That must mean something. And yet she wasn't saying it with any emotion or sense of enquiry. It wasn't intended as an invitation for me to open myself up to her. I think she was simply recognising the fact.

I was telling a friend of mine about this and she said to me: 'If you had been like that stranger in Paris and handed your mother a photo of yourself, what would it have looked like?' The question stopped me in my tracks. What would my photo have looked like?

And then, as I thought about it, it occurred to me that maybe we're really all going around like the man in Paris – handing out photos of ourselves that don't reflect what we look like on the outside, saying, 'Look, this is me, this is the real me,' and hoping someone will finally recognise us.

IF ONLY . . .

It seems to me we can never give up longing and wishing while we are thoroughly alive. There are certain things we feel to be beautiful and good, and we must hunger after them.

George Eliot

What is something you have longed for, or wished for, in your life?

I grew up within earshot of the docks in Liverpool, England. We could hear the low bellowing of the ship horns from our backyard. Lying in bed at night as a child, I wished that one of those ships would one day take me to a place far, far away – maybe even as far away as Africa.

Ours was a street of neglected council houses full of families shoehorned into small, damp rooms and poorly lit spaces. But my family was given special consideration. I was one of thirteen children and finding suitable accommodation for a family of fifteen was a nightmare for any council bureaucrat. Eventually, we scored a large house at the end of a row. We had four bedrooms and a sleep-out at the back. There was a long, narrow backyard with some fruit trees and a woodshed, but only one toilet. However, the post-war years of the 1950s was a time of rapid rebuilding. Some of the houses in our row were unoccupied as they were scheduled to be demolished and replaced with the hope of the future, the high-rise housing estates. This was a time of high adventure for the kids of our neighbourhood. We played war games in abandoned buildings or cowboys and Indians in overgrown factory yards or the decaying community hall.

I was the fourth child. My mother, with a stern look on her face, short curly hair and a floral apron with red piping, sported a new baby on her hip for most of my childhood. Apart from looking after the baby, she was always busy washing, sewing, mending, ironing and cleaning. She was a devout Catholic and accepted God's will without question. She had sworn in front of her priest and God 'to love, honour and obey' her husband, and she remained true to her vows. Her faith was so strong she offered up a novena – that's nine days of prayer – to the Infant of Prague statue after the birth of each child, asking the golden-robed child Jesus to protect her own child.

Did I love my mother? This is not the sort of emotion I can tease out from the tangled mess of feelings I experienced growing up. When you are part of a very large family, you have little contact with your parents. I had two older sisters and they were the ones who told me when to go to bed, when to wake up, when it was time for school or time for mass on Sunday. Others in the family were always vying for our parents' attention. I didn't. I was the stubborn one. I can say that I admired my mother. I respected her because she worked so hard. And I was aware that she worried all the time. Money was her primary concern. There was never enough. Sometimes there wasn't enough money for food. My mother was a proud woman. She did not like going to the local authorities to beg for family support. So not only did she have thirteen children to care for – including my youngest brother, who was intellectually impaired – she worked in an assortment of jobs outside the home, first as a social worker for a Catholic charity, then as a counsellor in a hospice.

The first inkling I had that things were not quite right was on the weekly rent day. Once a week, the housing agent would drive to our street, park his car by the kerb and impatiently sound his car horn. He expected all the residents to turn out and pay their rent through the driver's-side window. I was quite young when I first understood that we didn't always have the rent money. We were told to quickly pull down all the blinds in the house and stay quiet, pretending there was no-one home. This was quite a feat for a family of our size, but when you are terrified of being kicked out onto the street, you quickly learn to stay deathly still until the threat has passed. As this ritual was repeated week after week, I began to understand that we were not wealthy. We didn't own a car. The one battered bicycle in the family belonged to my father. We were very poor in a poor neighbourhood. There was, however, a reason for our poverty. My father drank.

He was not a constant drunk, but rather a weekend alcoholic. My father worked as a typesetter for a newspaper. His father had died when he was eight years old and I think a part of his problem stemmed from his father's death. My father was a very intelligent man. There was no word he couldn't spell. And he loved opera, especially the Italian operas. While his three older brothers received a university education and went on to be very successful and relatively wealthy men, my father had had to leave school early and go to work.

As soon as my father collected his pay on a Friday, he went to the nearest pub with his pay packet and stayed there drinking until closing time. My mother never received all his wage, which she desperately needed to feed her brood of thirteen. Actually, I have left out a significant detail: my father didn't go straight to the pub; he stopped on the way to buy the meat for the week, a side of mutton which we called a hogget, the cheapest cut of New Zealand lamb. Was it really from New Zealand? Probably not. The source of this meat was a mystery and we knew not to ask questions about it. When my father went drinking, he often left the hogget on the train on the way home from the pub. As little kids, my sister and I had to go to the station and ask the stationmaster if anyone had found some lost meat. The conductors and the stationmaster soon got to know us, and whenever a hogget turned up in lost baggage, it was immediately returned to our station for collection. My sister and I would struggle home, bickering and complaining while lugging the stinky carcass that sagged one way and then another and almost dwarfed us.

We dreaded Friday night, because that was the night our father drank himself stupid, and when our father drank, he turned nasty. Very nasty. He became a violent man. He would stagger through the front door smelling of beer and work himself into a rage because someone had left dirty shoes or a beaten-up cricket bat in the hallway. If you gave him cheek or answered back, he would lash out at you. If he was displeased with our mother, he would hit her – and I mean he would really punch her. We kids hated to see our mother hit, so a gang of us, whoever was around at the time, would jump into the fray and try to protect her. This jumble of arms, legs and screaming kids would bump into walls and stumble into the hallstand. My father would throw us off, belting each of us in turn, and then stagger into the lounge room where he'd collapse onto the old horsehair couch and fall asleep.

I was the angry, feisty one. I was not about to put up with our mother being hit. I didn't care what happened to me. I only wanted to save her. I'd often charge into the scuffle and end up being thrown against the wall. I'd go to school the next day with bruises on my arms and face. This went on for years, yet the nuns made no comment. The next day our father would be subdued and contrite. He'd sit at the kitchen table in silence, still wearing his white work shirt, grey trousers and braces. He might mumble a few words as he leaned his elbows on the linoleum-covered kitchen table, drinking his tea from a cracked cup, but it was hard to know if he was apologising or still complaining.

Christmas Eve loomed like an ominous threat in our house. Dad's behaviour at Christmas was particularly frightening because he started drinking during the daytime. We'd go to mass and listen to the soaring beauty of the Christmas hymns. That's one thing we Catholics get right. We sing to joy. Our Christmas hymns lift your spirits. The priest would talk of 'peace on earth', which was something we did not understand. We would take communion. The thirteen of us sat in line in a pew with our mother, rugged up in our hand-me-down winter coats. We felt safe there; church was our sanctuary. I would pray: 'Please, dear Jesus, stop our dad from drinking.'

When I was ten years old, Dad came home from visiting one of his wealthy brothers for a drink on Christmas Day. The usual fight broke out in the hallway until he made his way to the couch and slept off the rest of the day.

The next day, as Dad was chopping up the Christmas tree in the backyard – we needed the wood for the fire – I couldn't help myself: I gave him some lip. I knew it was dangerous. But how dare he ruin our Christmas! It was the one day we hoped our family could be normal. He belted me with the part of the tree he was holding. All those prickly branches lashed my arm and cheek like a cat-o'-nine-tails; the pine needles pierced my woollen jumper leaving red-spotted welts that looked like a rash. I didn't cry. I wouldn't give him the pleasure.

Not being able to handle the drink was one of the blights of our Irish heritage. But Dad also suffered from that other curse of the Irish: melancholia. So he was angry when he was drunk and, more often than not, miserable when he was sober. Yet there were also dazzling times when he was the most amazing man on earth. When he was in a good mood he was a showman. He'd stand on a soapbox at the back of the house and sing Italian operas to his ready-made audience in his beautiful tenor voice. So there were moments in my childhood when I felt content. Fleeting moments.

The real magic dust sprinkled on my childhood was the freedom to roam. We explored the neighbourhood and beyond at every opportunity. Our parents didn't seem to worry about us. The only time they expected us to turn up was for meals. I suppose they would have noticed if one of us went missing, but that never happened. This didn't mean we were safe; it meant we managed to survive. At ten, I was the leader of my local gang, which included some of my younger siblings. If we were playing cowboys and Indians, I was either the Indian chief or the head of the cowboy posse. We'd ambush other kids playing in the same abandoned building. We'd pelt them with bits of rubbish, sticks and stones and anything else at hand. Rotten fruit was a particular favourite, but rare.

In general, fruit was eaten before it ripened on the tree. You got used to the bitter tang of unripe apples. One time we set fire to the next-door neighbour's backyard. We probably didn't mean to set the place on fire, but the real campfire outside our imaginary teepee got out of hand and the flames leaped across to some broken furniture and then the woodshed. I sometimes suspect that I could have become a criminal, because burning down a neighbour's backyard seemed like no big deal. Not when we were kids.

The abandoned community hall was the perfect meeting place for local kids. It was so far from our house we felt as if we were going on an expedition to a foreign land. I'd take my gang on adventures around the hall. The mesh-covered windows set high in the walls were all broken. The rays of light beaming through these high windows gave the dusty interior an eerie atmosphere. There was a stage at one end and some broken chairs at the other. It was a spooky place because of the ghosts. The hall had once doubled as a local theatre and we believed the ghosts hadn't left the theatre just because it was abandoned.

As it turned out, there were evil spirits haunting the hall, but they were very much alive. A paedophile lived in our street. I know the word now, but none of us knew it then. He was a skinny, pimply-faced nineteen-year-old. He had a bike and he would volunteer to take us for rides. A little girl in the neighbourhood told me that he took her to one of the old sheds at the back of the community hall and asked her to do certain things to him. So the next time I saw him taking her for a ride, I rounded up the gang and we followed them to the shed. We were very careful to avoid being seen. We were Indian braves hunting our prey! Besides, we wanted to spy on the creep. We saw enough. Basically, he wanted the little girl to give him a blow job.

I went home and told one of my older sisters. The story must have gone up the chain of command in the family, for the next thing I knew a detective arrived at our house to ask me questions, which in those days caused quite the neighbourhood scandal. My father was so outraged he made me pray to Our Lady of Purity every night. Then I was sent away to stay with our grandmother for two terms. Later I found out why. I had to go to the children's court as a witness. The most fabulous part of this experience for me was getting new clothes. I had always worn hand-me-downs from my older sisters. Now, for the first time in my life, my parents bought me new shoes, a new coat, a new hat and matching gloves. New shoes! I kept looking down at my feet in their shiny new school shoes. I put on that coat and admired myself in the half-moon mirror hanging over our mantelpiece in the lounge room at every opportunity. It was brown with a velvet inset in the collar. I looked like little Princess Anne, I thought.

The courthouse was an old building with lots of policemen and people dressed in their Sunday best. I was taken into a courtroom. It looked like a church without Jesus on the cross. The judge asked me: 'What was wrong about what Stanley did?' I answered, 'Pulling down your pants is a sin against God.' That's all I could think to say. Stanley got off. He continued to sexually abuse the local children. Most of us knew to keep away from him, but he'd always manage to find some new victim. Stanley ended up driving the school bus because a local priest vouched for him. 'Stanley's all right,' he insisted. 'He's turned to the Lord.'

Another of our adventures involved riding Dad's old bike to the docks. There would be two of us on the bike, one pedalling while standing up and the other sitting on the seat. Then we'd change places. I'd stand on that dock, breathing in the diesel-laced salty air and gazing up at the great black wall of a cargo ship in front of me, and I'd think: One day I'll sail the world on a big ship like this.

We were full of cheek. I'd call out to a seaman, 'Hey, mister, will you take us over the ship?' And some weathered deckhand would invite us aboard. These tough, tattooed men were always very kind to us. They'd take us up and down ladders to different decks. We'd see the thudding engines in the engine room. The tour inevitably ended at the kitchen, where the cook fed us a meal without complaint. I was always hungry. There were migrant kids from Italy and Hungary at our school. The other kids made fun of them for eating smelly sausages and cheese, but I didn't. Sometimes a migrant kid would give me one of their sausage sandwiches at lunchtime.

The greatest influence in my life – and I think it was this that saved me – was the theatre. My mother came from an artistic background. There were actors, musicians and authors on her side of the family. Every Christmas, the kids of our street would put on a nativity play. We'd make the costumes ourselves. One year I made Joseph's beard out of my sisters' Modess pads. We were so naive. No-one ever told me what they were for. The nuns were vague on matters of reproduction. They lectured us: 'Girls! When you go to the bowl room' – this was how they referred to the toilet – 'you do *not* go with a friend.

You do *not* hold hands. You do *not* touch each other. It's a private matter.'

Old Aunt Annie left a piano to my mother. I took it over. I taught myself to read music and play the piano. I knew that instrument inside out. I knew every key. I could take it apart and reassemble it blindfolded. That's how much time I spent with that piano. At ten years of age I auditioned for a crowd scene in an opera company and won the part. From that moment on, and for the next eleven years, I was wrapped in this protective cocoon of theatrical types: divas, homosexuals, child actors, stage mothers, ugly panto aunts, classically trained thespians – the entire glorious, gregarious, grease-painted troop. Entering the theatre was like crossing a portal into an entirely different world for me; a world full of exotic and colourful creatures. I met some wonderful, wonderful people who took the time to talk to me and explain some of the facts of life.

I struggled at school. No-one knew about dyslexia in those days, so I had to teach myself to read as best I could. The nuns at St Bernadette of Lourdes were also violent. We'd be punished for talking in class, even whispering. So I got belted at home and belted at school. Sister Philomena slammed a desk lid on my head one time for not paying attention. Another time I had to kneel with a wastepaper basket on my head and pray. God only knows why. But I knew that I was musical. I dreamed of being the lead actor in a show. I knew I had the talent. My parents had other plans, however.

When I was twelve I started to cook for the family. I was being groomed to take over from my older sisters, who were both planning to leave home and live in a nurses' hostel while they trained to be nurses. A girl was needed in the home to help with the domestic chores and, since I wasn't good at school anyway, I was the obvious choice. To head off any objections I might have, my parents started a campaign to undermine my confidence. One nun told my mother: 'That daughter of yours is hopeless at schoolwork.' My mother repeated this to me constantly, and often reminded me of my shortcomings. Clearly, there was no point me continuing my education.

Cooking for a family of fifteen in a poky little kitchen with no bench space, an old wooden table, a pilot-lit hot water geyser over the enamel sink and the fridge in another room is no small enterprise. Just peeling potatoes for a family of that size leaves your hands red and numb from the cold water. Often that was all we had to eat for our meal. Potatoes. Our mother would go to the one grocer who occasionally allowed her to buy food on credit and come home with four pounds of potatoes. I would cook us all chips in dripping for tea.

Meanwhile, I was feeling increasingly distant from my family. One time I overheard my parents talking; my father was complaining bitterly about me. I felt totally rejected and unloved so I ran away and hid in bushes at the end of the street until dark. After hours of hiding, I made a decision which has stayed with me for life. 'Okay,' I said to myself, 'you'll just have to look after yourself. Do what has to be done yourself. That's how it is.' When I got home I discovered no-one had noticed I was missing. To me, that marks the day I drew away from this world I lived in and from my family.

This feeling grew stronger as I grew older. By the time I was a teenager I couldn't bear even to sit in the same room as my father. I loathed him. Instead, I spent as much time as I could at the theatre. For a long time I had been wary of getting close to people – people close to you hurt you. But the theatre people were so warm and kind, they melted my resistance. They became my first real friends, my alternative loving family.

At seventeen I was allowed to get a job to bring more money into the home. I worked as a dental assistant. The dentist was the funniest person I'd ever met. We laughed so much. He even had his patients laughing, spitting and half choking with laughter as they lay in the chair with their mouths full of instruments. Discovering that some people could approach life with such a sense of fun made my home life seem even more miserable.

I was desperate to leave home, but my mother begged me to stay. When I was 21, my mother had to go into hospital and I was expected to run the house. Mum pleaded with me not to bait my father, to stay quiet and keep the peace. I couldn't do it. One night Dad came home drunk, yelled at us kids and then kicked the dog. That was the last straw for me, him kicking the poor dog. I picked up a carving knife and threatened to kill my father. I thought he'd get angry, but he just said: 'You stupid, stupid girl. I want you out of this house tonight.' I couldn't leave that night, of course, as Mum was still in hospital and the younger kids needed me; I had to wait one more very long week. But my mind was made up and, as soon as our mother came home, I left. A nurse I knew said I could flat with her. I organised a van and took all my furniture. I'd bought it myself with the money I earned as a dental assistant, so there was no way I was going to leave it behind. 'You did it, girl!' I said to myself. 'You finally did it. You got away from them.' But that was not entirely true; I worried constantly about my younger siblings.

From the time I was a small child listening to the ship horns blasting from the docks, I had longed to travel far away, and that was what I did. Eventually I moved to Australia, where for several years I worked for the Royal Flying Doctor Service in the Northern Territory. Wherever I lived, I joined the local theatre group. Eventually, I got the lead in one rather saucy production in Darwin. I can remember walking down the main street one time and seeing a group of boys gathered around a poster pasted to a wall. 'She's a bit of all right,' one said. The others agreed. When I got closer I realised they were looking at a poster advertising the upcoming theatre production – and that it featured a scantily clad portrait of me!

I finally realised that I was not ugly or stupid, but I was still wary of letting anyone get close to me. But one man proved particularly persistent, and eventually I relented and married him when I was 26 years old. I chose a good man, one who was the opposite to my father in every way. I was also determined to be a totally different kind of parent to my own children. I had two children within two years and then we moved to Brisbane. I didn't know anyone in my new home and felt so alone. I kept looking in the mirror and asking, 'Is that me?' I couldn't recognise the person staring back at me. And I couldn't stop crying. My husband urged me to get help, and I found a doctor who picked up a box of tissues and handed them to me, saying, 'You've got postnatal depression.' It was such a relief to discover I had a medical condition and it wasn't just me being hopeless.

The pills the doctor prescribed didn't work for me. In the end, it just took time and a lot of talking. One of the things that helped me through this difficult patch was my faith. The Catholic Church has always been important to me. I love the rituals: the smell of incense, the ringing of the communion bells, the chanting and blessings. I love it partly because it is the most wonderful theatre, but also because I am spiritual. When no-one else loved me, Jesus did. And I felt that love, really felt it. I believe in Jesus and he gave me the strength to save myself. This filled me with gratitude. When I recovered, I joined with a local priest to start a self-help group for mothers with postnatal depression. These groups expanded to include support for a variety of mental health issues.

Outside the official session times, I'd have desperate mothers knocking on my door at home, saying things like, 'Have you ever felt like carving up your baby with a carving knife?'

'Yes,' I'd reply, adding: 'Come in.'

I'd invite the mother and her baby in and talk to them, while also keeping an eye on my own children (I had three by then). These self-help groups multiplied until we were running ten groups around Brisbane. I saw understanding in these groups – love, too, in the way the members supported and cared for each other. And I saw miracles. Hearing other women talking about their lives and talking about my own life, I came to understand that forgiveness is the greatest miracle of all.

My parents came out to visit when I was in Brisbane. They'd never travelled anywhere, so flying all the way to Brisbane from Liverpool was an extraordinary event. I planned special meals and outings with the children.

My husband was wary, as I had told him about my childhood and how it had been affected by my father's alcoholism and depression. But I was used to dealing with all types of mental illness now, and I felt confident I could handle this situation. I met my parents at the airport, and it struck me that we were not a family that hugged one another. My mother wasn't exactly the maternal type. The only time we ever hugged, were actually physically affectionate, was when my father died some years later.

My mother was still vibrant and active, but my father looked old and frail. His heavy drinking days were over by this stage, curbed by ill health; he died not long after he made this trip. Seeing my parents again brought back so many memories and emotions. There were so many things I wanted to ask my father. I felt that he was, at the core, a decent man. So why did he drink? And why did he drink until he became violent? Was he jealous of his brothers? Angry with his parents? Did he even know he was violent? But these are not the sort of questions you can ask when you are first reunited after a long absence. So I acted out the role of a warm and loving daughter who was pleased to see her parents. And, indeed, I was very pleased to see my mother. I introduced them to the children and we drove back to our house.

That evening, I was chatting away with my mother as we prepared the evening meal when my husband came home and asked where my father was. I hadn't noticed his absence, but it seemed my father had wandered off somewhere. We looked all over the house, but we couldn't find him. Finally, I looked in the garage, of all places. I found him curled up on the back seat of my car, crying.

'What's wrong?' I asked.

'I can't forgive myself for what I did to you,' he said wretchedly.

This came as a total shock to me. First, it meant that, all along, he'd known what he was doing. And second, I realised, he wanted my forgiveness. At that moment, I realised how far I'd travelled from my painful childhood.

'Dad,' I replied, 'I've let that all go. I forgave you years ago.'

That was the only conversation we had about my childhood and the only conversation I needed.

The young girl who had stood wistfully on the Liverpool docks looking up at those big ships had finally sailed away from all the anger, fear and humiliation of her old life. But it wasn't boarding a ship and crossing an ocean that enabled me to put my old life behind me. The true journey took place when I found my way to forgiveness. It didn't come easily, but when I reconnected with my parents in Brisbane all those years later, I discovered something profound: it was through forgiving my parents that I was at last truly set free.

THE HARDEST THING

What, for whatever reason, was the
hardest thing you learned to do?

The hardest thing I had to learn was how to deal with the impotent rage that stalked my every thought when juggling work, family and the demands of caring for a very sick child.

My daughter's illness arrived by stealth. Maybe it began when she was ten years old, maybe eleven. I can't say. I just know that she began to slip – slowly at first, very slowly – into the grip of anorexia nervosa. You would think that alarm bells would have rung, given all the news headlines and media commentary focused on the problem of eating disorders in young girls. Yet I failed to see its looming shadow. Why would my child get an eating disorder? Besides, I was preoccupied with work commitments, the routine of an active family – school drop-offs and pick-ups for my daughter, after-school activities – and the demands of running a household.

By the time she was twelve, the 'puppy fat' my daughter loathed had melted off her and she was growing tall. Still, she asked me to serve her smaller portions of food. When I ignored this request, she left the unwanted food on the plate. Maybe, I thought, I was serving her too much food now that she had slimmed down.

I first became consciously aware that something might be wrong when she started drawing plates and indicating how much food should be put on them. She even specified how many peas – ten at first, then gradually less. She was counting peas. But I was still in denial. 'She's being a typical teenager fussing over food and trying some sort of weird diet she read about in a teen magazine,' I told myself. 'She's just doing what many adolescent girls do.'

However, it wasn't only her eating habits that were changing. Her behaviour was too. There were arguments. Slammed doors. Sulking. It was bewildering at times, but this was normal behaviour for an adolescent girl, wasn't it? One time, when her brother was away on a school camp, my husband and I decided to take our daughter out for pizza. She went into her room to get dressed. Her father and I were ready to leave at 6.30 pm. At seven she was still in her room. We yelled at her to hurry up. By 7.30 pm. we insisted that it was time to leave; it didn't matter what she was wearing. Sour-faced and unimpressed, our daughter marched out the door to the car, where she slouched in the back seat and sat in sullen silence for the time it took us to drive to the pizza restaurant.

As soon as we were seated in the restaurant, our daughter stood up again, announcing that she had to go to the bathroom. Five minutes passed. Ten. She didn't return. We ordered pizza – a margherita, the plainest pizza possible, which was all our daughter would eat – and I went to look for her.

I found her in the ladies toilets in tears, trying to scrub a scuff mark off her new dazzlingly white sneakers. There was no scuff mark that I could see. Wads of sodden paper towel were scattered over the bathroom floor. I insisted that she return with me to the table. Reluctantly, she followed me and slumped into her chair with her hands in her windcheater pockets. It was as if our daughter had disappeared and all that remained was a dark shadow of misery. She refused to eat any of the pizza.

Driving home from the restaurant, we did what parents tend to do in those circumstances. I delivered a stern lecture on appropriate behaviour. Her father backed me up and added a few more thoughts about working hard to put food on the table. Then, when he slowed the car as we approached some traffic lights, our daughter jumped out of the moving vehicle and ran off into the darkness of an inner-city park.

We were at first stunned, then terrified. Our twelve-year-old daughter had vanished into the night. We drove around that park for hours. At least, it seemed like hours. I have no idea how long we searched for her. My heart was clenched so tight I could feel the physical pain of it. We'd stop at some creepy path or deserted playground opposite the cemetery and call out her name, but there was no response.

Eventually, we found her standing beneath a lamppost at the edge of the park. It was well past midnight. We were so relieved yet still terrified. What tectonic plate had shifted in our relationship with our daughter that this could happen? But she had made her point clear. There were no more lectures on the way home that night. Even then, I attributed her behaviour to the fact that she was upset. I couldn't stretch my thinking to the possibility that my daughter was suffering from a more serious problem than mere adolescent angst.

I didn't mention her condition to friends until she was officially diagnosed as suffering from anorexia. Until that point I insisted that she wasn't ill, she was just a 'fussy eater' and 'picky' with food. Dealing with a fussy eater was a problem I could handle. The alternative – a diagnosis which would propel us both into the public domain of clinics, doctor's waiting rooms, hospitals and psychiatric wards – was more than I could bear. Admitting to myself that anorexia nervosa was a mental disorder took several more years. You never imagine when you watch your small child playing at the beach, say, that within a few short years she could develop a life-threatening mental disorder.

Once a diagnosis is made, though, the symptoms are unmistakable. An anorexic is not just underweight. She shivers all the time because she cannot keep warm. Her heart develops an irregular rhythm, confirmed by ECG. Her blood pressure is low. Downy hair appears on her face. Before the diagnosis I was acting like a 'normal' mother trying to encourage my daughter to eat healthy food. After her diagnosis I felt enraged at the world. I was angry with women's magazine editors for filling their magazines with fat-shaming photos of bikini-clad celebrities who had, allegedly, put on weight. We'd find these magazines in doctor's waiting rooms and even on coffee tables in eating disorder clinics! I was angry at all the 'low-fat' foods advertised on TV 'to help you stay slim'. I was angry at the ads for sugar-free drinks that not only kept you slim but promised you a fabulous fun-filled life. Anorexia and fun did not go hand in hand. I can't tell you how many times ads appeared on TV or in government-sponsored messages focused on the 'obesity epidemic', along with their dire warnings about health risks. These warnings cut deep because my daughter was listening to them. I wanted to scream at the TV: 'Shut the fuck up!'

Once the GP confirmed the diagnosis, I had a goal: I would make my daughter eat. I didn't go in for screaming matches over food, despite the great temptation, but I never stopped trying to convince, cajole, trick, entice her into eating something. Never. I was possessed. But still the days and weeks slipped by with no improvement. Then one day I drove her to school – she was in year seven – and watched her struggling to clamber out of the car and pick up her backpack full of school books. She was so weak she could barely stand straight. 'Get back in the car,' I said and took her home. She never went back to that school. I made an appointment to see the principal and her year-level coordinator and explained the situation. Her teachers were very sympathetic and sent her schoolwork to keep her up to date with her studies, but she couldn't concentrate.

My husband and I both worked from home, so we could look after her, but we were patrolling the boundaries of a disaster zone we couldn't access. I researched anorexia: its causes, cures, clinics, programs, hospitals, youth mental health facilities. I visited clinics to talk to staff. I thought this might be the path to take. One day, a couple of months after she'd stopped going to school, she simply stopped eating. No matter how much I harangued her, the only nourishment she would take was a third of a cup of milk a day. I was frantic. I booked her in to see multiple specialists. The first specialist we visited was a paediatrician at a nearby children's hospital. He told us he couldn't admit my daughter to hospital until she collapsed from starvation. He turned to her and said, 'Then we put a rubber tube down your throat and force-feed you.'

We booked her into a private eating disorder clinic for teens. She packed her bag and our entire family went to the induction interview. I got the feeling that the psychologist who interviewed us was trying to lay blame on the family dynamic. We thought we would be leaving our frail girl at the clinic – a prospect that made us desperately sad, but it was, we believed, our last hope. But that's not what happened. Instead, the psychologist announced that our daughter was too physically ill to be admitted to a mental health clinic. Not physically ill enough for hospital, too physically ill for the mental health clinic. Who would help our daughter? Now we had nowhere left to turn. No hope. I felt as if we had been condemned to watch our daughter die slowly of starvation. I could hardly contain my distress and rage.

We took her home. On arriving home from the clinic that had refused to admit our daughter, I rang a doctor friend. I was nearly hysterical by this time.

My friend came to the house and said to me bluntly: 'You butt out.' She told me I was not to watch what my daughter ate for the next few weeks. Then she persuaded our daughter to eat a little, just enough to stay out of hospital. Finally, I understood something quite profound: I could not control what was happening to my daughter. I could not eat for her. This was the hardest thing I ever had to learn: I could not fight the battle for my daughter. This was her demon and she had to be the one to face it down. And, to my immense relief and pride, she did. She was not cured overnight. In time, we found people, professionals, who could help her; professionals she trusted. But the same rule applied. They could not eat for her. She had to do the hard work herself.

In the meantime, I had my own demons to face, and it was hard work. I had to ignore my mother's intuition and give my daughter space. That was no small ask. We mothers always have our whiskers bristling, testing the air, noting fine details about our children – especially when they are ill. Our instinct is to hover. Are they well? Are they happy? Did they eat all their breakfast? Have they put on enough warm clothes? But in order to get through this ordeal, I had to back off. I could not fight the monster consuming my daughter; I could only be her cheerleader, calling from the sidelines: 'You can do it!'

Acting counterintuitively leaves scars on your psyche. To put your arm around your child's shoulders and feel you are hugging mere tissue paper and bone but do nothing; to conduct your life around a sick child without listening for the rattle of a biscuit tin or the tearing of a packet, any sound, any sign, that they are eating; to suppress the urge to listen outside the bathroom door for fear the illness has regrouped and emerged this time as bulimia, say; to face down the suffocating feeling that you are abandoning your child. It was a form of drip torture, one I lived not daily or hourly but minute by minute.

Yet my battles were mere skirmishes compared to the battle my daughter had to fight in the dark theatre of her own mind. While I wasn't aware what bits and pieces she consumed when she first started eating again, I do clearly remember the first proper meal she ate. We would have cooked, bought, ordered any food on earth that she wanted. She asked for Kentucky Fried Chicken.

Her father rushed out and bought a takeaway box with chicken, gravy and fries. She ate the lot. I cried, partly from relief, partly from exhaustion. After watching my daughter endure starvation for month after month I asked her, 'But weren't you hungry?' The answer devastated me. It still does. 'Yes,' she replied, 'I was hungry all the time.'

SURPRISING MYSELF

How ridiculous and how strange to be surprised at anything which happens in life.

Marcus Aurelius

What about your life has surprised you?
The surprises can be big or small, good or bad.

I am by nature an extremely positive and optimistic person. My children claim that if one of them was to lose a leg I'd probably reply, 'But you were so lucky that it wasn't your good leg!' This became a recurring joke in our family: 'Lucky it wasn't your good leg!'

Then, at 42, I found myself unexpectedly trapped in a strange universe. A fog slowly descended and swallowed my bright and shiny world. I could not explain what was happening to me, nor could I understand my own emotions.

The first wisps of fog blew into my life when, without warning, my mother was suddenly rushed to hospital. She needed an emergency operation to stem the flow of blood from a stomach ulcer. She was slow to heal, and so she went into respite care. At that time, I had a busy career, two young children and a husband who had his own health issues, but nevertheless I managed to visit her every day.

When it came time for the post-operative check-up, I had to change my work schedule so that I could pick my mother up from the respite care home and drive her back to the hospital. The check-up was a standard procedure.

My mother was 66 years old and quite fit, so I had no premonition of impending disaster. Besides, as I've said, I was a natural optimist.

To my surprise, when we arrived at the hospital, my mother wasn't able to get out of the car unassisted. I had to go into the hospital and ask for help. That's when I discovered we'd turned up on the wrong day to the wrong ward.

'Your mother is booked in to see a specialist in the oncology ward tomorrow,' the receptionist explained.

I couldn't quite get my head around the implications of this statement. I was more concerned by the prospect of having to return my mother to the respite care home and then do the hospital run through busy city traffic all over again the next day.

When I told the receptionist that my mother couldn't get out of the car, she made a phone call. 'It's all right,' she told me. 'They were able to move the appointment. They can see your mother today.' The receptionist kindly organised an orderly to accompany me back to the car park with a wheelchair, and together we were able to extract my mother from the car.

I remember so clearly walking behind the orderly as he pushed my mother down one long and strangely deserted corridor after another. I was wearing flat-heeled boots, and I recall the sound of my footsteps echoing down the vast empty spaces as we headed to the oncology ward. I sat in the waiting room fidgeting with my phone, but nothing could distract me from the strangeness of the situation. When my mother's name was called, I went with her into the doctor's office. As the doctor spoke, it was as if I was no longer in my body but was watching the scene from above. The words fell from his mouth and landed with a metallic clatter on the floor.

'The tests are back. Your mother has terminal cancer. I'm afraid there's nothing we can do.' Then he turned to my mother and added, 'But we can keep you comfortable, control your pain.'

My mother sat slumped in the wheelchair and nodded her head as if she'd known all along, but the diagnosis slammed into me as if I'd just been hit by a train. My mind whirled with questions. I had a job that involved public speaking, a young family, a busy life. How could I juggle all these demands and, at the same time, take care of my sick mother and watch as she died?

Well, I coped. Or, rather, I convinced myself that I was coping. What else could I do? I was blessed to have a sister who resigned from her job to look after our mother. My sister was expecting her first child at the time. This seemed a cruel twist of fate. We had been looking forward to a wedding before the birth. My sister had to postpone those arrangements, knowing that in place of her wedding we would instead be organising the unthinkable: a funeral. I'd take over the care of my mother on weekends as often as I could. This meant our mother could stay in her home for as long as possible. We encountered some truly empathetic people along the way. The local doctor who would sit at our mother's kitchen table and try to work out a strategy to ease some ugly new symptom. The palliative care nurses. The radiologist who did my sister's prenatal ultrasound. When my sister burst into tears, the radiologist took the time to find out why. My sister explained that, while she did not want to know the sex of the baby, she would like her mother to know before she died. So the radiologist typed up a letter and sealed it in an envelope. My sister handed over the envelope and when our mother opened it she exclaimed: 'Oh! It's a boy.' Then, 'Oh no! It's a girl. Hang on, it's a boy!' My sister had to laugh. That was so typical of our mother – always joking.

It was hard to keep up a brave front. Only two months later, our mother was admitted to hospital. She quickly lapsed into a morphine-induced haze. The days I spent sitting by my mother's hospital bed telling her I loved her passed in a blur. And then, inevitably, she died. There was so much to do in the immediate aftermath: the phone calls, the death notices, the funeral, the eulogies – I gave one – the cemetery, the funeral reception . . . I did everything that was required, but it felt like I was operating on autopilot. The reality had yet to sink in.

The following week, I revisited my mother's grave with my sister and one of my brothers to say goodbye properly. I felt I'd not really managed to choke out those words in the hectic weeks before her death. So I farewelled her out loud, standing in front of her freshly dug grave still adorned with flowers, and I promised to look after my younger siblings for her. I wept – and then I resumed my normal life, working and caring for my family, as if nothing had happened. I convinced myself, and I convinced others, that I was all right. I could conjure up a smile at will, and I showed that smiling mask to the world. Everyone assumed I was fine.

Months passed. Then, one morning, I just couldn't get out of bed. It was a Sunday, so there were no meetings or other commitments scheduled. I think I had finally allowed myself to collapse. I lay in the foetal position, sobbing. My husband rallied and took the kids out for the day.

And he did more than that: the next day he visited our local doctor on my behalf. The doctor suggested that this was more than a symptom of grief; he suspected that I might have depression. When I resisted seeing the doctor – it seemed to me like just one more thing to do when I was already feeling overwhelmed by my endless to-do list – my husband made the appointment for me and drove me to the clinic.

The first thing the doctor did was prescribe sleeping pills. This alone made an enormous difference. I hadn't really thought about the fact that I wasn't sleeping. I just lay awake in bed at night, my mind churning with dark and menacing thoughts – thoughts I couldn't even understand. When I did manage to sleep, I would wake in fright, dripping in sweat with my heart pounding, overcome by a sense of impending doom. I felt certain that some great disaster was about to destroy me, my family, my whole world. If I were a religious person, I would have taken refuge in prayer. Instead, I tried to make myself see things rationally. Of course I was not facing impending doom. I was lying in bed in leafy suburbia beside a snoring husband. So why was I experiencing such absurd emotions?

Slowly, I began to realise that this unsettled state was my new normal. I was constantly surprised by this dark, pessimistic new self. It posed a daily challenge to my perception of myself as perpetually sunny and cheerful. Where once I had been happy to engage with the world, these days if I walked into a shop and a sales assistant asked, 'How are you today?', I wanted to reply: 'Go AWAY!' or simply glare at them. Needless to say, I didn't do this. I usually replied: 'Good.' And that became my standard answer when anyone asked how I was doing. 'Good.' In reality, I was anything but.

I remember hearing a radio presenter talking about growing tomatoes in his garden and I burst into tears. I wanted to have a life like that; a life in which I had the time, the energy and the inner calm to nurture tomato plants. I didn't even have time to read the labels on the tinned tomatoes as I hurriedly threw cans in the trolley as I raced down the supermarket aisle. I lived in a universe far from one where people could rhapsodise at length about the finer points of growing tomatoes; I was in this other place, a universe of shadows and fear and exhaustion.

I tried to make sense of my state of mind by reading books on psychology, psychiatry, neuroscience. I began taking notes and scribbling thoughts in an exercise book. It was clear that I had indeed slumped into a numbing depression. I was emotionally empty, burnt out. Most distressingly, I had lost the ability to care. How could I care about anything or anyone if I couldn't feel anything? I held on desperately to those core connections: my love for my family and my friends. But the little things in life that once gave me joy – walking along the beach on a sunny day, watching children scream and chortle as they chased waves on the shore, feeling the warm sea breeze on my face and inhaling the salty sea air – didn't even register. I felt nothing.

I went back to the doctor, who prescribed anti-depressants. I was told these pills might take a few weeks to kick in, but they never did. I tried relaxation and visuali-sation exercises without success. I could easily visualise myself in flowing white gossamer-fine robes sitting on a moss-covered rock by a babbling brook in a peaceful glen, but my mind added the bloody annoying ants, mosquitoes and gusts of wind laden with allergy-inducing pollen followed by an invading army of evil dwarves. (Perhaps, I've seen too many *Lord of the Rings* movies.)

I scribbled down more thoughts in my exercise book. One had considerable traction. A commentator on the radio explained that goal setters were like a golfer playing on a never-ending course. As soon as he achieved the goal of putting the ball into the hole, he raised his head to look for the next flag. That was me. I was a goal setter. So I stopped setting goals and found that this gave me more room to manoeuvre. I lived my life from day to day, minute to minute, in much the same way that people did back before career planning, time management and an endless stream of emails made life hectic.

If I had known I would feel this numbness for eight years, I don't know what I would have done. My mother's death was bad enough, but one of my children fell ill a year or so later. It wasn't one of those illnesses that goes away. The illness manifested like chronic fatigue with multiple complications and it lasted several years. Once more I coped. I coped by mechanically doing all the things a mother should do. I was numb most of the time, but when emotions did break through I was swamped by a tsunami of rage, fear, hostility and despair. Obviously, I had to lock down these emotions, keep a tight lid on them; they were dangerous. That was the approach I took and I was very good at it.

I still marvel at the way I juggled a career, a family and day-to-day life by acting out what you were meant to do if you had a career, a family and a day-to-day life. But I couldn't see any alternative. My own health issues were way down the priority list. I had a sick child. My job involved acting cheerful and funny at conferences around Australia, when inside I was empty. If the audience was buoyant that gave me energy. I fed off their good spirits. If the audience was stressed or anxious, I could feel the gravitational weight of their anxiety pulling me down.

During my forties, which I think of as the Crap Years, I did have one pivotal experience. I was asked to address a rural women's support group in a country town that was enduring a long and devastating drought. I could tell some funny stories about growing up in a country town. But I was aware that there was an elephant in the room. I had to address the desperate situation these women were facing. I decided to open up and tell my real story in a raw and honest way. But how would an audience react to something darker and more emotional? I didn't know. All I could do was describe what it was like to be funny and cheerful on the surface while despairing and feeling bleak on the inside.

I began cautiously with some funny anecdotes. Then I switched from being an entertainer to instead speak directly from the heart. 'I live in the city,' I said. 'I don't know what it is like to battle for your livelihood, your way of life, your very survival through a long and unforgiving drought. The only experience that comes close for me are the years I spent dealing with a young child with a serious illness. And I can tell you this: that illness was the last thing I thought of at night; it was the first thing that leaped into my consciousness when I woke. It made me sit bolt upright in the middle of the night, overwhelmed by panic. It filled my mind so completely that I could drive the car from home to the supermarket with no memory of how I got there.

My mind was always jumping from one idea to the next, desperately searching for some answer, something I could do to solve this problem. But there was no solution.'

There. I had done it. I had spoken from the heart. And something magical happened. The audience was so still I could almost hear them breathe. I realised I had crossed a barrier. Humour is a powerful way of connecting with and energising an audience. This was different. I was engaging with each person in the room directly. My story wasn't their story, but it was a story about life, and the struggle to deal with the unwanted and unexpected. It had meaning and the audience could identify with it. What I was most struck by, though – and this changed the way I approached my work forever after – was that I didn't have to dazzle the audience with my wit or entertain them with hilarious anecdotes to hold their attention. I could speak the truth about the struggles we all share as we deal with the stress, the demands, the conflicts and problems that we all face in all our lives. I had discovered the power of stories, up close and personal stories.

This talk was cathartic for me. Even recalling it now is cathartic. I was not out of the dark woods at this stage, but a tectonic shift occurred in my psyche around that time. What I learned during that time was to hold the things you value close and let everything else slip away. Not caring about my hair, my house, my eyebrows, my weight, other people's expectations, my own relentless self-criticism, matching towels, career goals, ambitions for my children and other people's opinions was a good thing. I learned to prioritise what mattered to me. I learned that you cannot solve all problems, please all people or control all situations. So I didn't try. And a weight lifted from my heart. I regained some of my old lightness. This new way of thinking and living took time to perfect. After all, I had been trudging through life for the past eight years. Now, even the way I walked changed. I had a spring in my step once more. I was, as Charles Dickens would put it, 'recalled to life'. It was as if the world now sported a fresh coat of paint. Colours were brighter, birds sang in the trees. I'd forgotten about birds. When the sun shone, I could feel the warmth on my skin. I'd forgotten about sunshine. And for now, my family were okay. *I* was okay. And, believe me, okay is very good indeed.

MAKING IT THROUGH THE NIGHT

Many of us have experienced a 'dark night of the soul'. What person, experience, object or belief has helped you at a time in your life when you were trying to make it through the night?

I married just after graduating from university. Even before I married him, I knew I shouldn't, but every time I tried to break it off, he persuaded me to stay. And I soon realised that I had wed a childish, competitive, emotionally abusive man. I stayed for a lot longer than I should have. Why? The oldest of explanations: I had married my father.

My father and I had a very difficult relationship – he was constantly putting me down, deriding me, undermining me. The emotional cruelty and verbal abuse I suffered with my first husband all felt very familiar to me. And it's so easy for 'very familiar' to feel normal. When the marriage finally ended, the parting was not amicable, but it was a relief.

I had been divorced for five years and was living in Portland, Oregon, when I met the man who was to become my second husband. I was doing some volunteer work for a not-for-profit organisation in the inner city; he was the director there and was married to a lovely woman. I liked them both very much but I didn't see a lot of them. I moved on after a while and we lost touch. About four years later, I was in San Francisco for a conference when I ran into him again.

DORIS BRETT & KERRY CUE

He was bereft. His wife had died just a few months
earlier and the loss had felled him. We talked for a long
time, and he told me that he was finding it difficult even
to go to the movies by himself.

'I go to the movies sometimes,' I said.

He rang me not too long after and we arranged to see
a film together.

I wasn't thinking of it as a date – I'd only intended the
invitation as a friendly gesture – but, to my surprise, that's
what it turned out to be. We connected very naturally
and things progressed quickly to the point where we soon
realised we wanted to be together. I knew that he had
loved and still did love his wife, but he also loved me and
I felt very comfortable with that. I don't think you stop
loving someone just because they die. And I think that
the heart makes room for love when a new love comes
along after that death. It doesn't negate or minimise that
first love.

My husband-to-be suffered from rheumatoid arthritis.
He had pain every day and, although he coped well with
it, the reality was that it would get worse in the years
to come. When he asked me to marry him, it was a big
decision for me. I loved him, but I had been leading a very
independent life, and I needed to consider the fact that
I could end up looking after a husband in a wheelchair.
Our courtship had only been seven months – there really
hadn't been time to think through the challenges that lay
ahead. We went to his doctor together to talk about what
to expect for him health-wise. The doctor was very frank
in his response. While confronting, at least when I made
my decision I did it knowing the worst that could happen.
I said yes. I would marry him.

There was an unnerving aspect to loving and committing to someone who was likely to get much sicker. Usually when you enter a relationship you just assume without thinking that the two of you have a long and equally healthy future. In a way, though, it was like committing to life. We think we know what kind of lives we're going to lead, but in reality none of us knows with any certainty what's going to happen tomorrow, let alone next year. Anything can happen to anyone at any time, and most of us cope with that truth by denying it. A friend I talked to at the time put it very simply: 'Take your happiness where you can get it,' she told me. And I agreed.

Once I'd made the decision to marry, I was so happy. My husband was a wonderful man – he was smart and funny and kind. And he had so much wisdom. He had lived with a lot of pain from his arthritis for quite a while, but his attitude was: 'I'm in charge of it – I'm not going to let it hold me back.' He loved to cook and would splint his wrist so that he could chop and stir without pain. I would come home from work and there would be a cooked meal waiting.

At one time, after he'd had some surgery, he did in fact have to use a wheelchair for a few months. Oddly enough, that was actually easier for me when we went out. I could push him and we could just go. Prior to that, and afterwards, going out or walking anywhere was a very slow process. I had to slow my own pace right down to match his when we were out together.

After our marriage, we decided that he would move into my house and we would rent out his house. Combining two households required decision-making for both of us.

One of the things my husband brought with him to my house was a cabinet in which his first wife had kept her linen. It had an odd musty smell. I removed the linen and aired it out, but the smell remained – it was very distinctive and no amount of cleaning or airing could change it.

We put the cabinet in the living room, but I didn't store my linen in it; I'd always stored the linen in a cupboard in a different room, some distance away from the living room. One night, just after we'd married, I got into bed and immediately noticed that the pillowcases had that distinctive musty smell, even though they had never been near the musty cupboard. We both looked at each other, startled. 'Honey,' I said, 'she's just here to check that you're okay.' And with that, the odour disappeared from the pillowcases and from the cabinet, never to return.

We had been married for nearly eight years when my husband's pain, which had always been bad but manageable, began to increase severely. We were going back and forth between his two specialists – a rheumatologist and an internist. However, the two specialists never communicated with each other. The internist thought the extra pain was due to worsening arthritis but the rheumatologist wasn't sure. The pain kept increasing no matter what we did and we just couldn't get any answers. It was heart-rending seeing my husband in so much pain and so obviously deteriorating, and it was terrifying not to know the cause. I was so frightened of losing him, scared that he would just slip away while the doctors hemmed and hawed. I ended up contacting both doctors to ask them to please talk to each other so that we could work out what was going on. This finally prompted them into action.

The rheumatologist phoned me and said, 'I think your husband has cancer. And it's bad.' I was stunned. But I didn't say anything to my husband, because the rheumatologist was only speculating at this stage. Instead I went to the grocery store. I started crying in the middle of the aisles there. To my relief, no-one took any notice of me.

A few days later, after speaking with the rheumatologist, the internist ordered a bone scan. Afterwards, he called my husband with the results. It looked like cancer, he told him. Probably multiple myeloma. In answer to my husband's question, the doctor said that he probably had five years. Before he hung up, he arranged for my husband to come in the next day for further testing.

My husband got off the phone with the internist and, in a state of shock, asked me what he should say to his kids. I felt that he shouldn't say anything until the diagnosis was confirmed, and he agreed. He called each of his kids that evening just for a chat. After that, he asked me to go to the local store to buy him a bagel. Some time later, he said he was feeling unwell and would retire early. As I helped him into bed, he looked at me and said, 'I think I'm dying.' And then he collapsed.

I was desperate. I rang the internist, who said, 'Get him to the hospital as quickly as you can.' I called my stepson, who lived close by, and asked him to help me carry him to the car. My stepson came right over, but he said there was no way we could manage it on our own. I phoned the ambulance. The paramedics arrived quickly and tried to revive him before they took him to the hospital. At the hospital, they worked on him for another 45 minutes before pronouncing him dead. He died in my arms nine days after the rheumatologist called to tell me it could be cancer.

It was so hard to process his absence. I kept wondering: 'Where have you gone? Where is your essence?' It seemed impossible that he was there one minute and so completely gone the next. I was devastated. I missed him terribly. I still miss him now, nineteen years after his death. I still find myself wondering what he would have thought or said about issues ranging from daily news items to life crises.

In the Jewish tradition, for the seven evenings following a death, friends and family visit to share condolences and talk about the person who has died. It is called 'sitting shiva'. In some ways, it's like the Irish wake. For each of those seven nights, the house is full of people talking and reminiscing, many of them bringing cakes and savoury food to feed the stream of visitors. It is a ritual that has been practised for centuries – a way of sharing grief, supporting the bereaved and offering the human comfort of company. But as an introvert, all I wanted was quiet and space to be alone. The grief was overwhelming – I felt raw and vulnerable. I needed a quiet cave and instead my house was bursting with people, with noise, with lights; it was like being hit in the face. I couldn't stand it. I was constantly retreating to the garage, the bedroom – any place where I could be alone. A friend of mine came when I was at the end of my tether and I just pushed some food into her hands and said, 'Please, please, have something to eat. And then go.' I'm not sure she's ever forgiven me.

I was distraught – I felt absolutely hollow with loss. I forced myself to keep following my daily routines, instructing myself just to keep putting one foot down, then the other. It was almost more than I could manage. I would start to think I was coping, and then suddenly I would be overcome by a wave of grief and realise that I wasn't.

A few months after my husband died, a friend persuaded me to go on a wine-tasting outing with some other friends. We were just chatting as we had lunch – someone said something funny and I laughed. I was amazed. It was the first time I had laughed since my husband's death. I had thought I would never laugh again and this made me realise that I could. It was a milestone for me.

Still, I continued to miss my husband intensely. I was unnerved by the fact that he was wholly and fully here for years and then in an instant was not here. Not anywhere. At an intellectual level I knew, of course, the facts of death as well as the facts of life. I understood what happens at an organic level when a living being dies. But at an emotional level – an existential level – it seemed an impossible, and impossibly painful, puzzle.

Soon after the funeral, his son was at the house and we were sitting at the table with others. I had just poured some drinks for people. His son was having a whisky on the rocks. He put his glass down after taking a sip and the ice cube shot out of the glass and flew across the room. We all just stared in astonishment; the glass had not been put down with any great force. After a moment, my stepson laughed and said, 'He's here with us, letting us know how he feels about me getting into his best Scotch.'

Months went by. It was now ten months since my husband's death. I had been due to visit my doctor for a check-up, which included a blood test for the marker for ovarian cancer. My mother had died of ovarian cancer and she'd also had breast cancer, so my doctor felt that it was a good idea to have me tested annually. I'd had the reminder for the test sitting on my desk when my husband died and I had been putting it off. Finally, a pain in my hip sent me to the doctor's and I decided I might as well have the blood test at the same time. Soon after my doctor called to tell me the marker was elevated. But, my doctor added, I was perimenopausal and that could be a benign reason for the elevation. She recommended an ultrasound.

The radiologist in charge of the ultrasound procedure didn't sound too concerned. She thought that what she was seeing was benign, although she did add we couldn't rule out cancer.

My doctor was not taking any chances. She recommended surgery and arranged for a surgeon specialising in ovarian cancer to be present, 'just in case'. My heart rate went into overdrive. My doctor, aware of my anxiety and keen to save me the unbearable tension of waiting, managed to schedule the surgery for just a few days later.

The specialist did in fact take over during surgery, as it turned out I had ovarian cancer after all. It was considered early stage, but then there was some uncertainty as to whether it had spread. I was very lucky to be classified early stage, but the idea of it spreading was terrifying.

I joined a cancer support group. The doctor who ran it was concerned that I was still focused on grieving for my husband whereas I should be focusing on my cancer. But how do you do that? How do you simply decide that ten months have gone by and now it's time to stop grieving and focus on something else? It's impossible. You can't turn grief on and off like a tap.

Odd things happen when you're dealing with a cancer diagnosis. Decisions that you used to make without thinking suddenly become loaded with existential weight. The renewal for my magazine subscription arrived in the mail. Should I renew it for three years, as I normally did? Or should I opt for the safer one year? Screw it, I thought, I'll renew for three years, and if I'm not here in three years, someone can cancel it.

My oncologist told me that I would lose my hair. In fact, he told me that I would lose every hair on my body. And I did. In places where I didn't even know I had hair – the insides of my ears, for instance. Knowing that you are going to lose your hair is one thing. Actually losing it is another. There was no way I could have prepared for the shock of seeing myself as bald as an egg. I was devastated by it. It wasn't vanity. Or at least vanity played only a very small part in it. It was the shock of being not-me. I had already lost so many parts of my life and self, perhaps this was one loss too many. People said to me that it was 'only hair', but for me it wasn't 'only hair' – it was *me*. Once, when I was buying something in a department store, I had to show my driver's licence to the assistant. She just looked at me. Without my hair, I didn't look like my photo. What were people seeing when they looked at me now? I wondered. I felt that my body had betrayed me, and the way I looked was evidence of my body's betrayal. It made me feel ashamed.

The chemotherapy regime I was on was debilitating. I was exhausted and weak and I suffered from 'chemo brain' – the term popularly used for the cognitive fog that often accompanies chemotherapy. In the past, doctors used to dismiss it as anxiety until they realised that the cause was physiological and not psychological. I had it to an extreme degree. I couldn't even read a single page of a book. By the time I got halfway down the page, I would have forgotten what I had read at the top and have to start all over again. I would lose track of what I was saying in the middle of a sentence. And when I was tired, I couldn't even string the words together to start the sentence. I couldn't make decisions – not just major, complex decisions, but simple ones, such as: 'Should I buy more milk?' My brain's executive functioning – that part of the brain that plans and makes decisions – was off the job. Even two years after chemo ended, I still had chemo brain. It took a long, long time for it to resolve. Now, eighteen years later, I am close to my pre-chemo cognitive functioning but not completely.

In addition to chemo brain, I was also incredibly fatigued. Apart from the 'new normal' of continuing chronic exhaustion as the chemo took its toll on my body, I had what my oncologist called 'collapse fatigue'. I would be walking along, thinking I was okay, and then, without so much as a second's warning, I'd be so exhausted that I couldn't take another step. Friends who'd never had chemo simply couldn't understand this particular form of fatigue. Those who had experienced chemo understood it very well. Collapse fatigue never stopped feeling disconcerting. We are so used to reading our body's signals and getting advance notice of things that it surprised me every time.

All of this meant, of course, that I was in no position to be my normal, independent self. I lived alone. I was weak and I was sick. All my life, I had hated asking for help, but now I didn't have any choice – I had to do it. Most people were happy to help. There were a few though who said no to some request that would have required minimal effort on their part but would have meant an enormous amount to me. I was crushed by their refusals. I don't think they were even aware of it. For people unused to asking for help, making the request is an act of courage every bit as taxing as sky-diving or public speaking is for others. I wish I could have said to those people, 'Of course you have a right to say no, but please, do it gently – this is harder for me than you can imagine.'

During my cancer treatment, some friends simply disappeared and others, sometimes unexpectedly, stepped up. One friend came over every week to carry the garbage out for me. I was too weak to do it myself. She said it was nothing, but for me it was huge – I have never forgotten her kindness.

Another young woman, whom I barely knew, sat with me a couple of times during my chemo infusion. She was so tender with me. She had moved to America from England recently. Just before her move, her mother-in-law, with whom she had a very loving relationship, was diagnosed with breast cancer. The mother-in-law kept it a secret from her as she didn't want to hinder the couple's move to the United States. This young woman felt terrible about not being in England to support her mother-in-law through treatment. Perhaps in looking after me, a woman of her mother-in-law's age, she was able to feel a little better.

Some time into my chemo treatments, I decided to go to a gift fair in the city with a friend who owned a gift shop. While my friend checked out a supplier, I headed for a shop that sold hats and was browsing there when someone spoke to me. I looked up. A nondescript middle-aged woman was smiling at me.

'You're the reason I came,' she said, though I'd never seen her before. 'I wasn't planning to come to the city today, but I just kept being pulled here.' She continued,

'I have a gift.' She held out her hands; they were empty. 'Sometimes I can heal people with these hands. I knew as soon as I saw you that you were why I was called here.' She reached out and touched my shoulder. She radiated calm. 'You're going to be okay,' she said. 'You're going to be okay.'

I was close to tears. She had come here to tell me what I so badly needed to hear. It felt like a blessing. I'm not a particularly spiritual or religious person, but when she said those words to me and touched my arm, it felt as if she poured her energy into me. Every few years her business card pops up in odd places around the house – I have no idea how it gets into these spots, they are not my usual storage places – but whenever I find that card, I give her a call to let her know how I'm going.

Another time, in between chemo sessions, a friend and I decided to walk to a volcanic lake at the bottom of a caldera. It was a vertical hike of a mile or so. I was pretty sick at the time and didn't know if I was going to live or die, but I was determined to live while I was alive. The hiking was hard, as I was weak from chemo, but I really wanted to do this. At the bottom of the path is a scene of surreal beauty. The lake is sacred to the Indian tribe who originally lived in this area and it feels that way – there is a sort of magic about it. I dipped my hand into the water and put it on my neck. It felt very healing – almost as if there was some spiritual power in the water. Just being in that eerily beautiful place and soaking in the quiet, mysterious energy touched me deeply.

It's been more than eighteen years since my husband died and I was diagnosed with cancer. When I look back to that time of intense sorrow and fear, the things that most helped me get through those dark nights of the soul came from opposite ends of the spectrum. On one end were the small, practical kindnesses shown to me by friends and near-strangers. On the other end were those occasions when I seemed to be touched by something much more ethereal – experiences hard to put into words – that gave me the sense of being part of a mysterious and beautiful universe: the stranger in the hat shop, the lake at the bottom of the caldera. These two vastly different kinds of experience gave me much needed nourishment and strength. One fed my heart and the other my soul, both of which had been hollowed out by too much loss and pain.

If someone had asked me at any time during that journey what would help my healing, I don't think I would have known what to say. Answering in hindsight, I can say those two things were the most valuable: acts of loving kindness, however small, and the experience of wonder. The first would have made sense to me immediately; I think everyone knows intuitively that when you're bereft and suffering you need to feel loved and cared for. The second kind of experience, though, I would not have predicted. I'm not a particularly spiritual person, I would have said. And yet when I look up the word 'wonder' in the dictionary, all the definitions condense down to one description: 'a feeling of amazement caused by something beautiful or remarkable'. And when we're feeling only half alive – or even when we're fully alive – isn't that what we all need?

THE
SOURCE OF
KNOWLEDGE

The only source of knowledge is experience.

Albert Einstein

What experience changed you or gave you
knowledge in a way you didn't expect?

I understood the concept of justice before I ever learned the word. Not in the usual sense of 'it's not fair' – the catch-cry of children everywhere – but in a sense that was deeply strange and disturbing. I was a small child, and the whole experience lasted less than ten minutes, yet it has shaped me in ways that continue to the present.

I was six years old and, instead of being at school, I was home in bed with a cold. I loved school, but it felt luxurious to be lounging in bed all day with books and crayons freely available and my mother cosseting me with chicken soup and affection. The sore throat I'd woken with had eased to something barely noticeable, and the other cold symptoms were minimal. In fact, I was feeling remarkably well.

It was mid-afternoon and my mother was out the back doing the laundry. Both the house and the street were quiet. I was selecting crayons for a drawing when suddenly the silence was broken by a series of shouts. It was coming from the street outside our house. Although the voices were loud, the words they cried were indistinct; all that came through clearly was the tone. I could hear someone yelling in fear and pain while others jeered and laughed.

The laughter frightened me. Filled with malicious delight, it felt dangerous.

I was sitting up, trying to see through the window from my bed, when I heard the front door fly open. My older brother and a few of his friends torpedoed through, shrieking to each other about what they'd just done. High on adrenaline, they raced down the hall, through the back door, the garden and out into the laneway.

No-one had noticed me as they passed. I was still sitting up in bed, trembling with shock, trying to process what had happened. There was an odd feeling of unreality about it – things like this were not supposed to happen – and yet at the same time it also felt horribly real, even hyperreal.

Suddenly the front door shook with a series of violent bangs. And then, as if whoever was out there hammering on the door had just found the bell, the house was filled with an intense clamour as someone stabbed the button repeatedly.

The sound finally reached the laundry. My mother came rushing down the hall. She passed my room too quickly for me to see her face, but I could hear her emotions in her footsteps. She was panicked – no doubt terrified that something had happened to one of her family members. That was the only thing that ever caused her to panic.

She opened the door and immediately I heard a woman shout: 'Where is your son!'

It was not so much a question as a demand.

'He's not home from school yet,' my mother replied. I could hear the relief in her voice even through her puzzlement. This was not someone come to tell her that her son was hurt. She didn't know, of course, that he had run through the house to the laneway only minutes before.

'Where is your son!' the woman shouted again.

And this time my mother heard the distress in her voice. 'What's wrong?' she asked, her voice full of concern. 'What's happened?'

'Your –' The woman's voice broke. She stopped, took a breath, and tried again. 'Your son was throwing stones at my son, *who is blind*!' The last phrase was screamed in rage.

'No! He wouldn't do that!' My mother's voice had risen now too. And then, more softly, she continued, 'I'm so sorry. That's terrible. But my son wouldn't do that. And he's not even home from school yet.'

Their exchange carried on for a few more minutes, the woman on the doorstep insisting that it was my brother who had assaulted her son, my mother insisting that it was impossible: he wasn't home and, in any case, he would never do such a thing. Eventually there was silence. There was nothing left to say. The woman strode away abruptly. I only saw her back from the window, but I could imagine her face. My mother walked slowly back down the hall, stopping at my bedroom door to look in. 'Are you all right, darling?'

I nodded.

'I won't be much longer with the laundry,' she promised. 'I'll bring you some jelly for your throat.'

I nodded again. And I said nothing.

And I continued to say nothing about what I'd seen.

That evening my mother took my temperature. 'Back to normal,' she said, stroking my hair.

But nothing was back to normal for me.

I look back now, amazed at the six-year-old who knew exactly what had happened and said nothing. It would have been so easy to tell my mother what I'd seen. To tell her that the woman was right. That it had been my brother and his friends throwing stones at the woman's blind son. And laughing. And running. And getting away with it.

My brother was a bully. I knew that only too well because I was a daily target of his bullying. It had always been like that and, perhaps because it had always been like that, it seemed like normal behaviour to me. None of my friends had older siblings, so I had no point of comparison. I simply assumed that all older siblings bullied their younger brothers and sisters – that it was the natural order of things. But this, what I had just witnessed, was different. I felt the difference in every cell of my body. It wasn't anger, it wasn't fear – it was an emotion I had never felt before, intense and unnerving. It was horror. How could someone throw stones at a blind boy, run away laughing, and then come home at dinner time to be greeted with a hug and a warm meal as if nothing had happened? What kind of world did we live in where this was possible?

Up until that time, my knowledge of the world had come from the stories that are told to six-year-olds: the classic fairy stories in which bad things may happen but good triumphs in the end; the Enid Blyton books in which magic may get you into trouble but courage, goodness and cool thinking will get you out of it. I lived in a world of happy endings, which was all the more striking because my parents were Holocaust survivors.

My mother had been born in Hungary, my father in Czechoslovakia. As Jews, they had been caught up in the horrors of the war in Europe. They had both been sent to concentration camps and were the sole survivors of their families. After being liberated from the camps, they met, married and chose to start a new life in a country far from their previous lives. They had few possessions to bring with them and a new language to learn, as well as all the adjustments required of the displaced. But all that permeated our home was gratitude and appreciation for Australia, the country that had taken them in. They loved Australia with a passion and were both determined not to inflict their past on their children. They never spoke of Europe and what had happened to them there. They walled it off and they did it so successfully that it was not until we were teenagers that my brother and I had any real sense of what they had been through. We were mostly incurious about their past; we focused instead, in the narcissistic way of children, on our own present. Our parents were loving, warm and stable – that was all we cared about. We had only the most limited understanding that they had been through a war the Germans had started and that they had survived to begin a new and good life in Australia. When my father once mentioned to my teenage brother that he would never buy a German car, my brother responded by scoffing at him and telling him to let the past go. My father said nothing. We really were ignorant.

This ignorance made it all the more shocking when, at six, I suddenly encountered evil – though I didn't yet have the language to articulate it. It had happened here, in front of my own eyes, in my own small world. And I was the only one who knew. The blind boy had not seen the attackers and my mother hadn't believed the accusations of the blind boy's mother. I was the only one who knew the whole truth. I had heard the blind boy's cry and I had also heard the triumphant laughter and jeers of my brother and his friends.

Even at six, I understood that my knowledge of the truth carried a responsibility with it. I had to decide what to do with this knowledge. I was on fire with the injustice of what had happened. I wanted fiercely to protect the blind boy. Equally fiercely, with a young child's simple sense of what was right, I wanted to see the aggressors punished appropriately. But there was something I wanted even more: I wanted to protect my mother.

I wanted to protect my mother from knowing what her son had done because I knew that knowing would be devastating for her. Young as I was, I already understood that what happened between my brother and me was too painful for her to acknowledge. His bullying was constant, vicious and unremitting, but I had stopped appealing to my mother for help – it was clear that she found it impossible to confront, and equally impossible to punish, one of her children. As an adult, I can understand that she had seen far too much hatred and violence in her life – so much so that the thought of it being present in her own home, in this sanctuary away from Europe, would shatter her. As a child, I didn't understand this, of course, but I was aware of the need to protect my beloved mother in this instance. I knew that if I told my mother what I had seen and heard she would realise that the blind boy's mother had been right. It would be impossible for her to deny what her son had done. And I knew too that she would be horrified by it. My mother took care of people, she was generous, compassionate – a natural helper of the weak and the sick. I took after my mother in this. I brought home stray dogs and rescued kittens from drains. I hated seeing the helpless suffer. The thought of those stones hitting the blind boy made me feel physically sick. And I knew that my mother would feel the same. To know that her son had been the perpetrator would be devastating. And so I said nothing. I must have made the decision within seconds and I felt absolute certainty about it. I had witnessed something terrible and I had to protect my mother from it.

Years later, I was sitting in a university tutorial, discussing the question of punishment and the concept of evil. I had obtained the marks necessary to get into medical school and was urged in that direction. But I didn't apply. I knew that I could never learn to give injections or to carry out procedures that would cause others pain. I enrolled in a social work degree instead.

'Are we all capable of evil?' the tutor asked us. 'Given the right circumstances, could any of us commit an atrocity?' Psychologists had famously directed the public's attention to these ideas. Experiments conducted by Stanley Milgram of Yale University (the results of which were outlined in his book *Obedience to Authority*) and Philip Zimbardo's Stanford prison experiments had shown that ordinary people could inflict pain and commit sadistic acts given the right circumstances.

The head-nodding in the classroom was almost unanimous; I was the only one who demurred. I was unsure. I had read the same studies as the rest of the group and I pointed out that not everyone in the studies had ended up inflicting pain or degenerating into sadistic behaviour. I was argued down. But even as I was argued down, I knew there was something more, something else, I wanted to say – I just didn't know how to articulate it.

A few months after that, I graduated and began working in my first job in a major hospital. The consultant psychiatrist who headed my unit specialised in, among other things, forensic psychiatry. He had just given a lecture on the clashes between the legal and psychiatric definitions of insanity. Among the sleep-deprived interns and medicos, I was possibly the only one who had stayed awake to ask questions.

My contribution had obviously been noticed and appreciated. The next day, the psychiatrist approached me, carrying a manila folder.

'Your questions yesterday were excellent,' he told me. 'I think you'll be interested in this.' And he handed me the folder.

The cover was blank. There was no title or descriptor. I had no idea what it was.

'It's from a case I was an expert witness for,' he said. 'A murder case. We got the murderer off on insanity without him falling clearly under the current legal rules for insanity.' He paused and gestured magnanimously. 'Take the folder home. Read it and then I can tell you how we argued the case.'

I put the folder in my bag and forgot about it while I did my day's work. That evening, I pulled out the folder and started reading. I will never forget what I read.

It was the personal journal of a man who had tortured, murdered and mutilated at least one young child. He was suspected of more but those allegations were never brought to trial. He had been fantasising about committing the atrocity for a long time and then he had done it. He was arrested while washing the victim's blood off his clothes.

The segment of journal I had been given spanned months of his fantasies about torturing children and described the delight he would take in watching their prolonged agony and eventual deaths. The fantasies were detailed and lasciviously described. Bloodcurdling didn't begin to describe them. Nothing described them. When I tried to think of the words, they came nowhere near encompassing the horror of what I was reading. What I was reading was alive. Horribly, terrifyingly, shockingly alive.

I wanted to rip those pages into tiny pieces. I wanted to burn them to ashes and then bury them. And I wanted to wash myself – to shower for a long, long time. I felt contaminated, soiled even, by exposure to this man's written words. But I read on. I read on because of the little girl – the one he did go on to torture and kill. To turn away would be akin to an act of cowardice. I owed it to that girl to read all that she had been forced to endure.

I was in a shaken state when I returned the journal to the psychiatrist the next morning. He was eager to discuss the case and immediately began to describe the legal and psychiatric gymnastics it had taken to get the murderer off on the grounds of insanity, despite the fact that he was not clinically insane. It had been ground-breaking work, he told me. It was clear he was proud of his cleverness. I hardly listened. All I could think was: 'This man exists. He is alive on this planet. He is flesh-and-blood, living-and-breathing real.'

In my late teens, I had sought out and read the memoirs of Holocaust survivors. I was trying to understand my parents' experience; they seldom talked about it and only with great reluctance. As a result, I knew only the barest of details: that they had been in some of the most brutal concentration camps and had both miraculously survived. Although there was no way I could imagine enduring the horrors they had endured, I at least was able to gain some sense of what they had been through. The survivors – the writers of the memoirs – were real people to me. My parents and their friends, who had been through similar experiences, were real people to me.

With the perpetrators, it was a different matter. In historical terms, I could see them as a group – the Nazis, the SS – but as individuals, they were like sketches, stick figures. Malevolent, of course, but abstract, like academic knowledge. I had never read a perpetrator's account of their inner experience. I had never heard a perpetrator speak of what they felt as they inflicted pain, torture and death. It was impossible for me to truly imagine them. And I had not even realised how the limits of my imagination had kept them remote from me.

But now, after reading the diary, there were no more stick figures. I had been propelled, unwittingly and unwillingly, into the mind of a monster – and the monster was real and sickening in his vitality. I wanted the stick figures back. I didn't want to know that people like this really existed. That desire to un-know was there in my wish to demolish and burn the man's diary, to shower and wash myself clean of any trace of him or his words. To keep myself far, far away from his horrifying reality.

And I suddenly recognised that, decades before, I had experienced a very faint echo of this – as a six-year-old listening to the jeering laughter of the blind boy's tormentors, their sheer glee at the distress they had caused. The feeling of unreality had been the same, the shock, the wish to deny that something like this could happen. Those two tormenting facts wrestling each other: This cannot exist. This does exist.

It was the first time I had witnessed my brother's bullying as an outside observer. When it had happened to me, it was too close to see clearly and dispassionately, and some part of me always felt that perhaps it was my fault, perhaps I wasn't good enough, worthy enough, perhaps something about me deserved his cruelty. But as an outsider watching from my bed that long-ago afternoon, it was totally clear to me that the blind boy was innocent; he had done nothing to deserve the abuse. I saw it, and I could not un-see it. It was a shock of knowledge: the first time I recognised that I lived in a world where someone could take pleasure in inflicting pain on another – not in the flush of rage or righteousness or retaliation, but purely and simply because it was delicious.

I never did tell my mother what I had seen that day, but I told my best friend at the time. She was as horrified as me. And then we didn't talk about it. Over the years, the rawness of the experience was varnished over. The intensity of what I had been forced to understand faded to a distant, abstract knowledge. Until I read that journal. And then it came back to me, magnified a thousandfold.

That journal changed me. In the course of a single evening, I went from someone who had not believed in capital punishment to someone who would, if I had been appointed the judge in this case, unhesitatingly have handed down the death sentence. In addition – and this was astonishing to me, as someone who turned my face away from screen violence and could not stand even reading about violence to animals – I knew that, if I had been required to do so, I could have pulled the trigger, loosed the trapdoor or pressed the button. I knew that if the situation necessitated it, I could even have administered the fatal injection. I would have hated doing it, would have physically recoiled from the act, yet I wouldn't have hesitated. I wanted him gone from the world.

As a child of Holocaust survivors, I thought that I had more awareness than most people of the existence of evil. I knew what had happened in those terrible times. I knew what the perpetrators had done. And yet, in reading that diary, I realised that my knowledge had only ever been abstract. The 'knowing' that I felt after reading that diary was different. Evil was alive for me. It breathed and had flesh and blood. The word that kept coming to mind was 'abomination'. It was a word I associated with fire-and-brimstone religious rants. But it was the right word. In reading that journal, I, a non-religious person, had come face to face with the devil. He was real. He lived in my world. And I could never un-know it.

THE
INEXPLICABLE

[The] only courage that is demanded of us [is] to have courage for the most strange, the most singular and the most inexplicable that we may encounter.

Rainer Maria Rilke

Have you had something inexplicable happen in your life?

We were crossing the Persian Gulf in a traditional Arab dhow in 1974 when I was struck by an overwhelming and inexplicable sense of foreboding. I was 24 years old and travelling with my husband through the Middle East from Jordan to Saudi Arabia. We'd been on the road for ten months. The trip had turned into an insane odyssey early on: first, because skirmishes that would eventually lead to a civil war were breaking out around Beirut, intensifying ancient hostilities throughout the Middle East; and, second, because the company we booked our travel through went bankrupt. Abandoned in Amman, Jordan's capital, we had continued our journey by public transport. When we arrived at the coast near Khafji, on the border between Saudi Arabia and Kuwait, we had decided that a voyage across the Persian Gulf in an old wooden dhow would make for an exotic twist to our adventure.

The dhow was large enough to carry two cars in the hold and two on the deck. The crew members, a mixed band of men from various local tribes, were clambering over the deck, shouting and waving anxiously at each other in languages we couldn't recognise. We handed some officials our passports as we climbed aboard and stumbled awkwardly along the listing deck, avoiding agitated crew, the occasional goat and odd crates of cargo. I felt a sinking sense of unease in the pit of my stomach. Something was not right.

The first problem was the cargo. We quickly realised by the way the crew yelled at us if we strayed too close to particular crates that this was no ordinary cargo but contraband of some sort. God only knew what. Hashish, perhaps? There was a group of glassy-eyed hippies sprawled on some old carpets in front of a ramshackle cabin mid-ship. We kept our distance from this peace-man band, even though they were the only other Westerners on board. The next problem was the toilet facilities. There were none. A barrel placed over a hole in the stern was the onboard solution. Passengers were meant to climb into the barrel and squat over the hole while clinging to the barrel's grimy insides. And this was a 36-hour voyage!

Suddenly, the tide changed direction, surging in and around the dhow's hull. It shifted. The sails rippled into place in the wind. We were on our way – without our passports. Fortunately, a kilometre out to sea, a launch came alongside and handed our passports to a crew member. The cargo might not be legal, but at least we were.

The first part of the trip was invigorating. We perched on some grain sacks and watched the dhow clip across a calm sea as a cool breeze carrying the smell of salt-brined air gently ruffled our hair. Night fell fast and the temperature plummeted. We put on all our clothes and huddled by some sacks of grain, but we couldn't stop shivering. Then a Pakistani passenger came over and offered us a seat in his Mercedes on deck. Warmth! Shelter! We were so grateful.

Somewhere in the middle of the gulf the wind dropped.

The sails fell limp. We were becalmed. When I looked out the car window I couldn't see a thing. The dhow had been swallowed by a thick fog. I climbed out of the car to see what was happening. The night was so still I could hear the tinkling of the brass chimes decorating the rickety cabin. I could hear the sails flapping listlessly and the sea washing against the dhow's hull. Then I heard another sound. A low rumble. That was all. Just a rumble.

Crew members sprang into action. Their shouts sounded like thunderclaps. They were frantically trying to hook lanterns onto the bow and masts. Suddenly, the bow of a massive cargo ship loomed out of the fog. I looked up at this monster towering over our heads and realised it was heading straight for our dhow. I froze and waited for the sound of metal crashing through wooden planks. In those few seconds, I relived a lifetime. Then, miraculously, the great wall of steel slid past us and left our dhow bobbing in its wake. I should have felt relieved, but I didn't. I felt completely unsettled. Even at the time I knew that the ship was a metaphor. Some deep inner fear of mine had materialised in a vision, a dark shadow looming over my life. How did I know this? And what was the threat? I had no answers. My faith in this vision was inexplicable. And why did I feel such a strong sense of dread after the fact? Nothing had happened. We arrived safely at our destination, yet days later I still sensed a menacing presence in my life.

I had first become aware of this inexplicable sense of foreboding while travelling through the bare deserts and ancient cities of the Middle East.

Months before our voyage on the dhow, we'd travelled from Amman to Petra by taxi. This journey was an extravagance, but the only alternative at the time as there were no hire cars or bus services. The four-hour journey along the potholed road in a decrepit vehicle with open windows for air-conditioning and a metal roof radiating the desert heat was nearly intolerable. Yet the discomforts of our trip instantly evaporated as we reached the outskirts of the fabled ancient city.

We left our backpacks in the hotel and walked via the small gap in the ravine known as the Siq into the archaeological wonder of the Rose City. Entering this canyon of temples and tombs carved into pink sandstone cliffs is like taking a journey into your own imagination. Petra is both strange and fantastical. One minute your mind is reeling as if you have entered a children's storybook and you half expect that, like Ali Baba, you might stumble across a cave of treasures. The next minute you feel uneasy, as if you are walking in the company of a ghostly presence among the stone walls of this lost kingdom.

After we'd photographed many of the sights, my husband suggested we walk up one of the steep cliff paths for a better view over the city. I was a little hesitant, as I am terrified of heights. However, I gave myself a good talking-to and pushed on. As we climbed higher and higher, my husband was nonchalantly pointing out various features of the city, oblivious to my growing distress. Then we arrived at a very tight bend in the path. There was no safety rail and it was a sheer drop down a God-help-me-I-am-too-terrified-to-look cliff face onto rocks below. My husband proceeded, unconcerned, but I backed away from the bend and clung to the side of the cliff face.

'Aren't you coming?' my husband called from up ahead.

'No,' I replied.

He turned and walked back to where I stood. 'What's the matter?' he asked.

'I can't get around that bend. It's the height thing. I'll stay here.'

'Oh.'

'Don't worry, I'll be all right,' I insisted, though in fact I wasn't all right.

'Okay,' he replied and continued along the path without me.

I was so angry with him. We'd been married almost four years at this stage. I expected him to be chivalrous and offer to help me around the bend, or at least express some sympathy, but instead he'd wandered off and left me alone. If he truly loved me, I fumed, he should have understood what I was feeling and offered to help. 'If he loved me,' I reasoned to myself, 'he wouldn't just walk off and leave me here.' With the benefit of hindsight, I realise that I was being a martyr and that it was ridiculous to expect him to read my mind. At the time, I was simply furious with him. Every now and again I peeked over the cliff edge and terror rekindled my rage. What I was feeling, however, was well beyond vertigo. I was feeling overwhelmed, immobilised by a monumental weight of fear and dread. The sense of foreboding was so powerful I could physically feel the crushing pain of it in my chest. It was later, on the dhow, that I understood these strong feelings were not caused by a fear of heights alone but rooted in some deep inner dread. But what was it? I swore to myself that I would return to Petra one day and climb that cliff. I would find the courage to confront all of my fears and do it.

*

The promise I made to myself took some time to fulfil, but in 2000 I had the opportunity to return to Petra. Entering the new millennium, I had two children, a career, and a husband who was both a good father and hard worker. But I was unhappy. Was it the marriage? My marriage was unsettled, perhaps. Incomplete? I couldn't quite put my finger on the problem. My children were now adults. My daughter had fallen in love with a Jewish boy and was living with him in Israel. Watching the news bulletins night after night, we became increasingly worried; the Second Intifada, or Palestinian uprising, had begun and the situation was extremely tense.

One night, while watching a news report on a particularly grim bombing in Jerusalem, I said to my husband, 'Let's go to Israel and see for ourselves if she's all right.'

My 'unchivalrous' husband immediately dismissed the idea. 'Oh no, it's far too dangerous,' he replied.

I gave him a look which should have been familiar to him by now. It meant: *You've got to be kidding me.*

'Fine,' I said. 'I'll go by myself.'

The next day I booked my flights. I also arranged a trip to Jerusalem, Amman and Petra. My daughter met me at Ben Gurion Airport with her boyfriend and they drove me back to his parents' house, where they were living at the time. I could see that my daughter was safe. While the situation had seemed alarming from the other side of the world, now that I was on the spot I could see that I had little cause to be alarmed. The security precautions taken by the Israeli police and secret service were such that it was extremely unlikely that my daughter would be caught up in an act of terrorism. Reassured, I advanced my travel plans and booked myself into accommodation in Jerusalem.

My daughter and her boyfriend volunteered to drive me there via the Dead Sea. We packed the car and drove into the Judaean Desert to camp overnight. This was a very relaxed time and it gave me an opportunity to talk to my daughter, although her boyfriend was always hovering nearby. But they were young lovers; I understood their desire to be together.

Night-time in the desert, with its profusion of stars glittering in the inky sky, is a spiritual experience. Your thoughts are expanded by the vastness of the universe and you realise it is so much bigger than your own little world. It lifts you out of yourself and you do feel a profound sense of gratitude to – what? The Great Void out there? – for your brief existence.

The following day we set off for Jerusalem. Looking at the map I saw that we would be passing the Masada ruins. Around 3 pm we stopped at the foot of the hill on which the ancient fortress stood. This was where the Jews took their last stand against the Roman Army in 73 AD and it is a site of great religious significance. There was a cable car to the summit and, although I was keen to see the ruins at the top of the mountain, I knew that the ride would most likely trigger my vertigo.

'I'd like to see the ruins but I'm afraid of going in the cable car,' I said to my daughter and her boyfriend. 'Would you come with me?'

'No,' the boyfriend responded immediately. 'This is a pilgrimage site for the Jewish people. We are only allowed to walk to the ruins.'

'I understand,' I said, 'but there's no way we would make it before closing time if we were to walk.' I turned to my daughter. 'Please, will you come with me in the cable car?'

My daughter looked at her boyfriend then shook her head.

'This is the last day we'll be spending together and we've had hardly any time alone. Surely it isn't too much to ask!' I protested.

Her boyfriend grew agitated, my daughter got upset, and I felt terrible. I spent the next hour apologising; I never did get to see the ruins.

Eventually we resumed our journey to Jerusalem. When we arrived at my accommodation the traffic was such that there was no time for a proper goodbye. I stood on the footpath and watched until the car carrying my daughter had disappeared from sight.

My room overlooked a walled garden paved in stone and landscaped with biblical plants. It was a beautiful outlook but I was in no mood to appreciate it. I rang my husband and cried down the phone for a good hour.

'He is her priority now,' I sobbed into the phone. 'I don't count.'

I was a miserable lump of grief that night. I wept and wept for what I had lost.

The next day, thanks to an archaeologist friend, I joined a group of Christian pilgrims from America. The small group was on an interfaith mission at a rare time when the Easter dates aligned across the Christian religions. I went with them into the inner sanctums of the Coptic Orthodox church and the Kidane Mehret Ethiopian Orthodox church for special Easter celebrations. My senses were overwhelmed by the richness of their interiors. There were ceiling domes painted with celestial angels, soaring columns and a host of golden icons of the saints. Then there was the chanting; so ancient, so otherworldly, so mysterious.

I had been feeling down, but these pilgrims lifted me up and carried me in spirit. This too was an inexplicable experience. It felt like a divine intervention. I was struck by the realisation that I was, for the first time in my life, doing something by myself. My life was my own and I was living it, actually living in my own skin. This was a profound revelation for me. I could do things by myself. I could be alone and make my own decisions. I had not experienced the almost floating lightness that comes with such freedom before. In the past any elation I might have felt was instantly crushed, overwhelmed by the extreme sense of foreboding I had identified on the dhow so many years before. This discovery was a long time coming.

I was born a twin. My twin sister was the dominant one and I lived in her shadow. My mother decided early on that I was sickly. I had pneumonia when I was young and she had already lost one child to pneumonia. So I was cosseted and fussed over as a child, but I was not given freedom to do things for myself. I did everything with my twin. I fitted in with her. Then, when I married, I treated my husband as if he were my twin. I did what he expected of me and what was expected by his mother and my mother. I did it automatically, without even questioning it. I put the needs of my husband and children first and lived my life for them because that was what was required of a good wife and mother.

The revelation I had in Jerusalem meant I could take a break from being a twin, a wife and a mother. I could just be myself. This time when I cried, it was for myself. I knew now that the shadow looming over my life, the inexplicable foreboding I'd first recognised 25 years ago, was my fear of being alone. When my husband walked on up the cliff face in Petra, leaving me behind, I felt abandoned and I was terrified. But I didn't have to be afraid anymore. I could be by myself. I didn't know how to be by myself – I would have to learn. But now I knew I could do it. I had to do it.

I travelled on to Amman and later a young driver took me to Petra. After sitting in the back seat of the car for a time, I made a decision: I was going to sit in the front seat and relish every moment of this trip. The driver was surprised by my request, but agreed. And when I asked him to put on some Arabic music, he pumped up the volume. The road had improved in the decades since I had last travelled along it. So had the air-conditioning. I thoroughly enjoyed taking in the view to the haunting Arabic soundtrack.

This time I had booked a guide to take me around Petra. Ali, a 42-year-old Bedouin, turned up at my hotel wearing a long white tunic, his head wrapped in a red-and-white keffiyeh. As he led me along the Siq, he began to describe all the wonderful sights we would see. I explained that I had visited Petra in 1974 – Ali would have been a youth at that time, I realised – and worried that I had made a mistake in booking this tour; I had already seen the tourist highlights.

Perhaps sensing my disillusionment, Ali changed tack. 'I think we should climb up the amphitheatre,' he said.

The steps of the vast amphitheatre had been carved into a cliff face. For someone scared of heights, it was a very steep incline, but what the hell, I decided – I'd do it. With a lot of puffing and sweating, I made my way to the top. As I turned to take in the view, Ali asked: 'Why are you carrying a walking stick?' I was holding a collapsible hiking pole.

'I need it to help me walk,' I replied.

'No,' he said sternly. 'Put it away.'

He took it from my hand. What did he have in mind? I wondered.

'See that?' he said, pointing to the cliff above the amphitheatre. 'We're going to climb up that cliff to the High Altar.'

'I don't think so,' I said, laughing.

'You came here to climb,' he insisted.

'You've got the wrong person,' I told him.

But he persisted. 'You came here to climb,' he said again.

Maybe this was fate, I thought, or perhaps it was a sign that I should let myself be open to new experiences.

'Okay,' I said.

We started to climb. The cliff face was steep, though not vertical, and we had to make our way up via rock ledges, cracks and carved platforms. Ali climbed ahead and then helped me up.

As we climbed he started to converse. Maybe he was picking up on the obvious cues – middle-aged, lonely, married, unhappy. Or maybe he had insights.

'Why isn't your husband with you?' he asked.

'Because he didn't want to come,' I said simply.

He turned and observed me. 'Why are there lines of tears on your face?'

I frowned at him, puzzled. I wasn't crying.

'You don't need those tears,' he added.

We arrived at another platform.

'Close your eyes and give me your hand,' Ali said.

I was wary, but I felt, somehow, that I was committing to my destiny. What was the worst that could happen?

I'd fall and my husband would have to come to Petra to collect my body. The prospect didn't bother me.

I closed my eyes. Ali took my hand and led me a few paces.

'Open your eyes,' he said.

I did, and found myself standing at the very edge of the cliff. I screamed.

'What is wrong?' Ali asked.

'I might fall,' I gasped.

'Don't you trust yourself?' he queried.

The question surprised me. Forgetting my fear, I thought about it, and I realised that he was right: I was in control of myself. I didn't have to fall.

As we continued our climb, Ali took me to the cliff edge several times, and each time there was a new insight.

'You need to let go of your children,' Ali continued. 'They are their own people. They have their own destinies. You have your own. Let go. Trust.'

I trusted Ali. The next time I stood on the cliff edge, Ali asked, 'What's a busy street in your city?'

'Bourke Street,' I answered, for I lived in Melbourne.

'And how do you walk in Bourke Street?'

'I just walk,' I replied.

'So just walk,' Ali told me.

The idea embedded itself in my brain.

'Just walk,' I said to myself over and over.

At last we arrived at the High Altar. The whole experience had been one of the most exhilarating and joyful of my life.

We returned to Petra by a different path. Later, I learned that we had climbed a much steeper and more perilous cliff than the one I had attempted to climb with my husband all those years ago. After the climb Ali took me to a Bedouin tent, where we drank tea and watched other tribesmen playing cards and music. Finally, he led me back through the ravine under the light of the stars to my hotel.

My mind was reeling from all the sights and insights of the day. I could trust myself to walk alone. This idea not only freed me, it freed my twin, my husband and my children to be themselves too.

To this day, whenever I am unsure of myself, Ali's words return to me. 'Just walk.' And that's what I do.

STARTING YOUR OWN SALON

In this chapter we'll take you through all the practical ins and outs of hosting your own salon. From the outset, we have always co-hosted our salon and have found that having two hosts has several advantages. It means we are able to draw on two different friendship groups for our salon participants and we can also act as each other's sounding boards when it comes to framing the discussion questions and considering who might be invited to the next salon.

We began our first salon truly not knowing what to expect. We hoped it would be a positive experience but were unprepared for how exhilarating, nourishing and life-affirming it turned out to be. All of the numerous succeeding salons have followed suit, with a wonderful mix of laughter, insight, compassion and the energy that comes from true connection.

PREPARING FOR YOUR SALON

Cast your net wide when you are deciding who to invite to your salon. As well as close friends, consider acquaintances, neighbours and work colleagues. We look for certain qualities in the people we invite and, equally, there are certain qualities that will make us feel a person is not a good fit for a salon.

Some of the qualities that don't mesh well with the salon philosophy are bossiness, a need to be constantly centre-stage, rigidity, self-righteousness and a tendency to lecture people.

We like to invite people who are open-minded, thoughtful, curious, able to listen and interested in hearing about experiences that may be very different from their own. Reflectiveness is also a quality that comes with the salon experience. We have found though that people who describe themselves as being unreflective – a 'just get on and do it' attitude – have loved the invitation, and the opportunity, to think about their lives and gain new understanding of its patterns and themes.

In a study on 'wise reasoning' published in January 2019, Professor Igor Grossman's definition of what wise reasoning was, included phrases such as 'a sense of humility . . . a recognition of diverse perspectives on an issue and an openness to integrate them'. He goes on to say that 'the ability to recognise the diversity in one's emotional experience may not only promote physical and mental health but also afford wiser reasoning'. The qualities he discusses are the qualities that people both bring to, and take from, the salon experience.

Once you have settled on the guest list, you will need to decide on two discussion questions, as they will be included with the invitation so that people have time to think about their responses. (There will be more on the discussion questions further on.) Written invitations should be sent a month or so before the salon. Sending a formal invitation sends the message that the salon is a gathering with a purpose, not just a casual get-together. As well as including details such as the date, time, location and the questions to be discussed, it's a good idea to give a brief outline of the salon's purpose and philosophy. Ours is as follows:

> *We are coming together in this salon to share our experiences and insights, and to discuss the joys, challenges and sorrows of life. While all topics are open for discussion, we will avoid defining ourselves by stereotypical categories of age, marital status, motherhood, career or any other label. We will meet on the philosophical plane where we can honestly express what we feel, think and understand about life in a safe, non-competitive and non-judgmental environment.*

Recipients are asked to respond to the invitation as soon as possible – numbers are limited and the host will need time to send out additional invitations if some of the original invitees decline. We have found between eight and twelve is the optimum number of participants (including the two hosts). We like to mix up the composition of the groups, so that no two salons have exactly the same mix of people in them, but you may prefer to have the same members present each time. Even in a group consisting of people who are close friends, the stories that emerge have often never been heard before.

A relaxed and intimate venue is preferable, as often the stories we exchange will be quite personal and emotional. We like to hold our salons at home, but you could meet in a cafe if there is a quiet room available; it's important that salon participants can hear each other clearly without having to strain or shout.

Our invitation suggests that participants might like to bring small sweet or savoury treats for the group, but makes it clear that this is optional, not a requirement. We also decided to support a charity through our salon, but once again donating is optional as we do not know the financial circumstances of every participant nor, indeed, what alternative charities they might choose to support.

THE SALON

We like to begin by thanking our guests for attending and then we explain the format of the salons. We also remind the group that the stories told are often deeply personal and emotionally charged, and it's possible that this is the first time the storyteller will have shared their story with others. Therefore, the salon must remain a safe space in which we do not judge or lecture each other. The stories should be treated as confidential and should not be repeated outside the salon.

The role of the host, or facilitator, is to ensure that each member has an opportunity to respond to the discussion topic. Your aim is to let the conversation flow, as some of the most astounding stories have emerged from the twists and turns of an unmediated discussion. That said, the facilitator also has to keep the conversation moving along and prevent it from degenerating into the trivial comments or complaints which are often a feature of everyday conversations. Finding the right balance between allowing the flow and directing the discussion becomes easier with practice.

Rather than moving in strict order around a circle, we

THE SUNDAY STORY CLUB

like to ask participants to share their stories in random order. We feel this adds to the sense of informality and ease. There will usually be someone who is itching to tell her story while others prefer to hold off until last. No-one should feel as if they are put on the spot.

In a new salon, the hosts should respond to the discussion questions first, to set a model for the pattern of timing and content. In subsequent salons, the hosts generally tell their stories last, although there is no hard and fast rule about this. Whenever there are new members present, it is best to ask more experienced members to speak first so that the new attendee can appreciate the variety of ways in which members respond to the same question.

One of the facilitator's tasks is a balancing act – to moderate the timing and pace of the stories. (The timing is discussed in a later section.) Some longer stories have the group enthralled, while other stories begin to ramble or don't take the audience with them. In the latter instances, the facilitator can diplomatically ask pertinent questions to get to the point of the story or gently move the speaker towards a conclusion. The co-host is very helpful here, both in judging timing and helping to refocus rambling stories.

The salon philosophy celebrates individuals and their unique narratives. In light of this, we ask members not to introduce themselves via their customary 'labels', such as full name, occupation and marital status. Instead, we've found that the best way to open proceedings – in which many members may be strangers or mere acquaintances (we do prepare adhesive name tags before each salon for easy reference) – is through the 'ice-breaker' question, which is generally something brief and playful. Each member introduces herself by her first name and then responds to the ice-breaker question. There is invariably a lot of laughter and nodding of heads.

For one of our salons, which happened to be held on the first day of May, we used this as our ice-breaker:

'Please tell us your name and how you would finish this sentence: *MAY DAY! MAY DAY! Send . . .*'

Here are a few of the answers we received:

'Energy.'

'A plumber.'

'Clarity.'

'Help . . . with marking essays.'

'More time.'

'More memory – for me, not the computer!'

'Sophistication.'

'Someone who can get rid of cockroaches!'

No subject is off-limits in the salons as censorship can act as a straitjacket. However, we have found there is one topic that instantly causes divisions: politics. In one salon, the discussion veered into a recent political scandal and we could almost see the room dividing along political lines. Some salon members moved in their chairs so that their posture was more withdrawn, more defensive. Others moved forward into a more aggressive stance. Others looked bored. We had to gently but swiftly shut the political conversation down and steer the group back to the original topic. If you are the facilitator for the salon and a political discussion erupts, you can move the conversation along with a reminder of the purpose of the salon, which is to talk about our lives, to be open about our flaws, virtues, successes, failures, triumphs and tragedies.

And we are here not just to talk, but to listen – respectfully and non-judgmentally. While participants are welcome to comment on others' stories – these comments can be witty, hilarious, moving or sympathetic – the responses shouldn't turn into a lecture. We once had a participant who took it upon herself to tell everyone else how they should be living, or should have lived, their lives. This is definitely not in line with the salon philosophy and we had to move the conversation on and away from her critiques. If you are the facilitator and a participant starts lecturing others, you need to act quickly to cut them off or other salon members may grow reluctant to speak. The freedom to speak openly and to be heard without judgment is essential if the salon is to be a success.

*

Our salon runs for two and a half hours. We chose to hold it on Sunday afternoons between 3 and 5.30 pm, with a half-hour break around four o'clock for refreshments. One hour is devoted to each discussion question. The facilitator must keep an eye on the time so that each member has a chance to respond to the first discussion question within the one-hour timeframe. Some responses will be naturally brief and others will be longer. Some of the longer stories will be holding the audience entranced and can be allowed to take that extra time. Other longer stories may be losing the audience or encroaching on the time needed for other people's stories. The facilitator can monitor the balance informally or, if you prefer, you could use something like an eggtimer or stopwatch.

We ask salon participants to turn off all devices. (There are, of course, exceptions to this rule – if someone needs to be contacted in case of emergency, they can leave their phone on silent.) Salon participants need to pay attention and really listen to the stories of other members. This deep listening is the powerful force driving the salon. We also ask that members don't read from notes when telling their story, as this detracts from the immediacy of the personal stories being told.

FORMULATING QUESTIONS

The questions that we ask in the salons are designed to open new and unexpected doorways into the participants' memory archives and to encourage them to explore their experiences from a new perspective. The questions can be imaginative, lyrical, thought-provoking or playful. They might invite the participants to envisage another life, visit a mythological place or imagine having been granted a magical skill or wish. They may ask participants to reflect on the obstacles, dreams or unexpected influences they have encountered in their lives. The questions are open-ended – they invite participants to ruminate on the decisions they have made, the attitudes and beliefs they have formed and the good or bad experiences that have shaped them. The questions are never confrontational, but rather invite participants into the discussion. We ask questions that sidestep the prepared narratives that participants often employ to explain their life experiences to themselves as well as to others. A salon member often discovers, in the telling of a story about themselves, that they gain new insights into their own history. These discoveries, be they heart-rending or heart-warming, are always surprising and revealing, and these stories often prompt the unexpected return of memories in others as well.

The idea sounds simple enough: ask a question, get an answer. But formulating questions that elicit meaningful responses is not as simple as it might seem. One phrasing of a question will get you a one-word answer, while a different phrasing of the same question will open up a whole narrative. Sometimes it's a matter of trial and error.

In one salon, we posed the following question:

> *Love is not love*
> *Which alters when it alteration finds . . .*
> William Shakespeare

What meaning does this have in your life?

When we formulated the question, we assumed that people would feel free to dissent from Shakespeare's assertion that true love should withstand all changes. Instead, we found that some salon members read these lines as judging them to be failures due to a divorce or broken relationship in their past.

In the light of this response, we amended the question for future use:

> *Love is not love*
> *Which alters when it alteration finds . . .*
> William Shakespeare

Do you think this is true or not? What types of 'alteration' might be sufficient to alter love? Has this had meaning in your life?

This rewording allows for the fact that Shakespeare's viewpoint is not necessarily the 'right' or only viewpoint. It also encourages further thought about what kind of alteration might lead to the loss of love – a circumstance that almost all of us have encountered in different ways in our lives.

We also like to ask questions that are somewhat unusual or quirky, as they encourage us to think outside the square. One example is the commonly asked question: 'What is your favourite book?' Instead of asking members to name their favourite book, we would ask instead: 'Why do you read?' This is a question many of us might not have considered before and interesting responses that involve self-reflection, rather than literary critiques, emerge. You, our reader, are reading this book right now. Why do you read?

Another question that encourages delving into one's life experience is: 'What is the hardest thing you had to learn to do?'

The answers ranged from:

'Controlling my readiness to anger in situations where it wasn't warranted.'

'Learning to be socially confident.'

'Standing up to my parents.'

'Learning to swim as an adult.'

'Travelling overseas by myself.'

'Changing my course of study from the one I was supposed to do to the one I wanted to do.'

'Leaving my marriage.'

Each of these responses brings with it a moving personal story.

As we have outlined above, after the initial ice-breaker question, we consider two discussion questions in each salon. We like to make the first question a lighter one and the second question deeper and more serious. We have learned, though, that we cannot predict the types of stories that will emerge; often the lighter question will invoke serious and intense responses while the more serious question will elicit some hilarious responses. This is one of the delights of the salon – the element of surprise. Salon members have often remarked on how much they love hearing unexpected responses to questions. We see things from perspectives that we would never have encountered. We think of things in different ways. We have our view of the world, family, love and friendship widened, and sometimes disrupted, in ways that enlarge us.

We have included some sample questions in the appendix that you might like to use when starting your own salon.

A DEEP BREATH OF FRESH AIR . . .

When we leave the salon, we often feel elated. The meaningful conversation, the camaraderie, the surprises, the laughter and the sorrows shared all contribute to this sense of elation. But the return of unexpected memories plays its part too. Perhaps we suddenly recall someone who was kind to us long ago. Or maybe we have put into words something about ourselves that we almost knew, but the information lay just out of reach in the shadowlands of our psyches. Our response to these discoveries is likely to be, as often happens in the salon, one of both surprise and gratitude.

Salon members will often email us after the session with spontaneous feedback:

It was the kind of stimulation and nurturing I needed after an intense time in my life.

Everyone in that room had a story and to be a participant as other women opened up and revealed aspects of their lives was truly awe-inspiring.

As I write this, more feelings are coming to the surface and what comes is the word 'safety'. I felt safe to reveal my inner thoughts and listen to others who also had a sense of safety. This was a special experience as I see myself as quite a private person and yet, with a group of near strangers, I felt I could talk about myself and feel at ease.

Thank you for a stimulating and engaging afternoon. What I like most of all is that people make me sit up and see alternative ways and views.

I had no idea of what to expect. As I walked out of the salon I realised I felt energised by my encounter with a new group of women and stimulated by our discussion.

The salon was a deep breath of fresh air. I felt hopeful and smiled all the way home.

APPENDIX

APPENDIX

W e have listed below a series of ice-breaker questions and discussion questions for you to use if you choose. There are enough questions to run twenty salons – that is, twenty ice-breakers and 40 discussion questions. You will notice that there are a handful of questions relating to a particular month or date. It can be fun to create a question based on the day or the month in which the group is meeting.

ICE-BREAKER QUESTIONS

Ice-breakers are the quick, unrehearsed questions designed to introduce group members to each other. We go around the group, saying our first name before responding to the ice-breaker question.

- Bucket lists are popular. But what about an anti-bucket list? Name something that you have to do but would like to stop doing now and never do again!

- What did you believe as a child that you no longer believe? Are you glad or sad about this reversal in your beliefs?

- You have died and mistakenly taken the elevator going down instead of the one that would take you up to the heaven you deserve. When you exit the elevator, what is the first thing you notice that tells you you're in hell rather than heaven?

- Dr Who has a sonic screwdriver that can fix anything. He has lent it to you for a single use. What would you fix?

- What is your soul food?

- The James Bond franchise has expanded to include Jane Bond. Imagine you are Jane Bond about to go on a mission. What one item for your use will you requisition from Q?

- You have been given the responsibility of writing the eleventh commandment. What will it be?

- *Reader's Digest* used to have a segment titled 'The Most Unforgettable Character I Ever Met'. Who is the most unforgettable or impressive person you have met or known?

- How old do you feel?

- In *Superwoman*, published in 1975, Shirley Conran wrote: 'Life is too short to stuff a mushroom.' How would you rewrite the line for a contemporary audience? *Life is too short to . . .*

- There is an old saying: 'You are what you eat.' Use this phrase to introduce yourself, but replace the word 'eat'. *You are what you . . .*

- Which historical era would you want to travel back to solely in order to wear the fashionable clothes of that time?

- Your skills are to be recognised by a National Honour Award. You would be granted the Order of . . . Fill in the blank. For example: the Order of Putting up with Annoying People.

- It's more than 50 years since the Beatles released 'All You Need is Love'. Replace the word 'love'. *All you need is . . .*

- You are astrologically challenged; you do not fit any star sign. You will have to invent your own unique star sign. What is the name, symbol and main trait common to that star sign?

- What is an annoying use of the English language that makes you roll your eyes whenever you hear it?

Date-specific questions:

- It's February, the month of St Valentine. Who would you like a Valentine's Day card from?

- Al Jolson famously sang about April showers. What would you like to be showered with in April or any other month?

- It is May and you have been elected lord mayor. You may issue one command to your citizens beginning with the words: 'You may not . . .' What is your command?

- The feast day of Russia's St Barlaam of Antioch falls in November. He was the patron saint of enduring miracles – but, alas, he was only a minor saint. What minor miracle would you hope for today?

DISCUSSION QUESTIONS

Your chosen discussion questions will be sent out with your invitations, so that people have time to think about them beforehand.

*

The most famous line in Tennessee Williams' play *A Streetcar Named Desire* is uttered by Blanche DuBois: 'I have always depended on the kindness of strangers.' Have you experienced the kindness of strangers in your life? Or, perhaps, the reverse?

*

You have been given the power to go back in time and tell one person one thing that will happen as a result of their actions. Who will it be and what will you tell them?

*

Criticism may not be agreeable, but it is necessary. It fulfils the same function as pain in the human body; it calls attention to the development of an unhealthy state of things.

Winston Churchill

The gentleman calls attention to the good points in others; he does not call attention to their defects. The small man does just the reverse of this.

Confucius

What role has criticism played in your life? Have there been times when criticism, either given or received, has had a major impact on you?

*

What is the best and/or the worst advice that you were given at any stage of your life?

*

The most courageous act is still to think for yourself. Aloud.

Coco Chanel

The *Macquarie Dictionary*'s definition of courage is: *the quality of mind that enables one to encounter difficulties and danger with firmness or without fear; bravery.*

Using either the dictionary definition or Coco Chanel's, have there been acts of courage, small or large, in your life? Alternatively, have there been times when you wished you had been more courageous?

*

One of the most beautiful qualities of true friendship is to understand and be understood.

Seneca

Can you expand on Seneca's definition? What do you look for in friends? Do your friends have any qualities in common? What aspects of personality would let you know that you would never want to be friends with this person?

*

We do not remember days, we remember moments.

Cesare Pavese

What are some (or one) of the unusual or special moments that stand out in your life?

*

The difficulty lies not so much in developing new ideas as in escaping from old ones.

John Maynard Keynes

Have you ever had to escape beyond the boundaries of an old idea?

*

Certitude is not the test of certainty. We have been cocksure of many things that were not so.

Oliver Wendell Holmes Jr

What people, events or things in your life have you been certain about, only to be proved wrong? What impact has this had on your life?

*

The truth will set you free but first it will piss you off.
Joe Klass

Have you ever learned the truth about somebody or some part of our culture that has pissed you off and/or set you free?

*

Not till we are lost . . . do we begin to find ourselves.
Henry David Thoreau

I'm not lost for I know where I am. But however, where I am may be lost.
A.A. Milne, *Winnie the Pooh*

Has there been a time in your life when you were lost – geographically, emotionally or spiritually – and how did you find where you needed to be?

*

Have you ever had a dream that let you know something important about your life or choices? Substitute a book for a dream if you are a heavy sleeper!

*

What is something you do that you know is irrational, and yet you keep on doing it?

*

If you could be present at one event in history, what would it be? And what would you do?

*

What is the object you would most passionately love to own? This passion could be rational or irrational.

*

The fairy godmother is able to make it to your birth – and she has remembered to bring her magic wand. She can bestow upon you one gift, and one gift only. What do you want it to be?

*

Name one clause in your personal 'mission statement'.

*

You have encountered a glitch in the space–time continuum which means that you have to live for the next six months in a TV series or film before the glitch rights itself. Which series or film would you choose, who would you be and why? (And don't worry: when the glitch rights itself and when you return to your real life, no time will have passed.)

*

Exciting news! The Mount Olympus Corporation has just announced that, for the first time in centuries, a position has been created for a new goddess. You have been chosen to fill the role. What will you be goddess of? What symbolic object or animal will be associated with you? And who would you like to sit next to at the gods' and goddesses' regular Sunday brunch? (For those unfamiliar with the Greek pantheon, please consult the Oracle of Google.)

*

The editor of a new book titled *Life Lessons: Accumulated wisdom* has asked you to be a contributor. What life lesson will you choose for your contribution?

*

In Philip Pullman's His Dark Materials trilogy (*Northern Lights*, the first book, was published in North America as *The Golden Compass*), each character has a deep connection with an animal that always stays near them. As the book progresses, we discover that these animals are in fact the individual's soul which, in this world, appears in external and material form as an animal. If you lived in the world of Philip Pullman, what animal would your soul be?

*

You wake up one morning delighted to discover that the Present Fairy has visited overnight and left you a gift. Her gift is the ability to invent something – the invention can be big or small and in any field. There is one provision, however: it should not be used solely for personal gain. What will you invent?

*

Dr Who has offered to lend you his time machine, the Tardis, so that you can go back in time to learn from, study with or interview someone for one whole week. Who will it be and what will you study or learn?

*

Dr Who has offered you the use of his sonic screwdriver for a very special purpose. As well as being a universal 'fix-it' tool of astonishing power, the sonic screwdriver can also be adapted to 'un-make' things so that they cease to exist. He has allowed you one opportunity to use it in this special capacity – what will you un-make?

*

Those of you who were enchanted by Enid Blyton's *The Magic Faraway Tree* as children will know that the tree is so tall that its branches extend into different worlds. Some of the worlds the children visit are: The Land of Do As You Please, The Land of Take What You Want and, less enjoyably, The Land of Dame Slap (Dame Slap being a tyrannical schoolteacher). Invent a world that you would like to visit at the top of the Faraway Tree.

*

It is said that 'seeing is believing'. What strange, bizarre, impossible or enchanting thing have you seen, or heard, that you would not otherwise have believed?

*

Zeus, Apollo and Hermes are arguing over the golden apple of Eris. Whoever is judged to be the best wins the prized apple. You are the judge and they are all offering hefty bribes – and you are open to bribes! Zeus is offering you absolute power. Apollo is offering you supernatural talent in poetry, music and the arts. Hermes is offering you unlimited wit and cunning. Who will you deem the winner and why?

*

The Pope has decided to anoint a new saint and bestow this honour on you. What is your saint's name and of what will you be the patron saint? (For example, St Jude is the patron saint of hopeless cases and lost causes.)

*

Do your clothes reflect your soul or spirit? If so, in what way? If not, why not?

*

I am the master of my fate. I am the captain of my soul.
William Ernest Henley

Do you agree or disagree? How has this manifested in your life?

*

Life is a constant oscillation between the sharp horns of dilemmas.

H.L. Mencken

What large or small dilemmas have you faced in your life? How have you resolved them and what impact has this had on your life?

*

When Romantic poet Percy Bysshe Shelley drowned in 1822 off the coast of Italy, his body eventually washed up on the shore near Viareggio. His remains were at first buried and then dug up and cremated on the beach in the presence of friends, including the poet Byron. His young wife Mary, author of *Frankenstein*, kept a relic from the funeral pyre which, strangely, did not burn. It was Shelley's heart.

Have you kept a memento to remind you of a loved one or someone you admire? Or have you kept a memento from a particular event or occasion? Why that particular memento?

*

In *Ten Poems to Change Your Life,* author Roger Housden described Mary Oliver's poem 'The Journey' as holding up a mirror to 'that moment when you dare to take your heart in your own hands and walk through an invisible wall into a new life'.

Have you ever had to take your heart in your hands and walk through an invisible wall into a new life? This change can be small or large, but must be one that required a conscious decision.

*

Rules are mostly made to be broken and are too often for the lazy to hide behind.

Douglas MacArthur

Has there been a written or unwritten rule that you have chosen to break? How did you come to this decision?

*

I have no special talents. I'm only passionately curious.

Albert Einstein

What is something you have been passionately curious about in life? Has this changed over the years?

*

'I remember where I was when I heard the news . . .' The 'news' that you heard, read or discovered, could be personal news or world news; small or large news, good or bad news, but with enough of an impact for you to remember where you were when you heard it. What was the news, where were you and what effect did it have on you?

*

You have to switch lives, and bodies, with someone for six months. It can be anyone you wish. Whose life will you choose to inhabit and why? And what will you do in those six months?

*

Adversity has the effect of eliciting talents which in pros-perous circumstances would have lain dormant.

Horace

Have you gained some knowledge, ability or talent through adversity which has been valuable to you in your life?

*

The month of March has been made famous by the quote from Shakespeare's play *Julius Caesar*, 'Beware the ides of March.' The ides of March – 15 March – is approaching. What have you learned to beware of in your life?

*

The holiday season is approaching with its rituals and festivals. This year you have been asked to create an entirely new festival. What would it be called and what rituals would it involve?

ACKNOWLEDGEMENTS

We would like to thank all the people at Pan Macmillan for the care and work they have put into *The Sunday Story Club*. Special thanks to Ingrid Ohlsson, who understood what we were about from the beginning and believed in us, and Danielle Walker, who has worked with us patiently and carefully to take the book through to its incarnation in print. We would also like to thank the wonderful Ali Lavau for her intelligent and thoughtful editing. And a thank you to our literary agent, Debbie Golvan, who shepherded the manuscript into the hands of Ingrid at Pan Macmillan. Thanks too, to Martin for the hours he spent for us, formatting a manuscript that contained way too many different kinds of font.

We would also like to especially thank the salon members whose stories are in this book – you know who you are and we appreciate your sharing some of the formative stories of your lives so very much.